Pause for Thought

edited by Joanna Scott-Moncrieff
from broadcasts on Radio 2 and Radio 4

British Broadcasting Corporation

Published by the British Broadcasting Corporation
35 Marylebone High Street, London W1M 4AA

ISBN 0 563 11996 9

First published 1971

Printed in England by Cox and Wyman Ltd,
London, Reading and Fakenham

Contents

Ash Wednesday

Family Living

Holy Week

Deepening Pleasures

Go placidly amid the noise and haste, and remember what peace there may be in silence. As far as possible without surrender be on good terms with all persons. Speak your truth quietly and clearly; and listen to others, even the dull and ignorant, they too have their story.

Avoid loud and aggressive persons, they are vexations to the spirit. If you compare yourself with others you may become vain and bitter, for always there will be greater and lesser persons than yourself. Enjoy your achievements as well as your plans. Keep interested in your own career, however humble; it is a real possession in the changing fortunes of time. Exercise caution in your business affairs, for the world is full of trickery. But let this not blind you to what virtue there is; many persons strive for high ideals and everywhere life is full of heroism.

Be yourself. Especially, do not feign affection. Neither be cynical about love for, in the face of all aridity and disenchantment, it is perennial as the grass. Take kindly the counsel of the years, gracefully surrendering the things of youth. Nurture strength of spirit to shield you in sudden misfortune. But do not distress yourself with imaginings. Many fears are born of fatigue and loneliness. Beyond a wholesome discipline, be gentle with yourself.

You are a child of the universe, no less than the trees and the stars; you have a right to be here. And whether or not it is clear to you, no doubt the universe is unfolding as it should. Therefore be at peace with God, whatever you conceive Him to be, and whatever your labours and aspirations, in the noisy confusion of life keep peace with your soul. With all its sham, drudgery and broken dreams, it is still a beautiful world. Be careful. Strive to be happy.

Found in old Saint Paul's Church, Baltimore: Dated 1692.

Efficiency

1. A SURGEON

How carefully do you check your monthly bills? Do you go over every item cheque by cheque, payment by payment, until you are quite sure that they haven't made a mistake? Do you believe your dentist when he says you need three fillings or do you ask to have a look for yourself? Do you trust your doctor when he says you need an operation or do you say, 'Why? show me the evidence'? The probability is that you don't question any of these things. You accept them on their face value and never doubt but that the statements you have been given are true. In my job as a surgeon the blind acceptance of most people never ceases to amaze me. 'Well, Mr Jones, you've got this blockage in your bowels. We'll need to cut a few of the tubes about – a plumbing job really. Very straightforward – we'll do it for you on Tuesday.' 'All right,' says Mr Jones, 'I'll leave it to you.' Total acceptance. All he sees are a few sutures on his belly. For all he knows I might not have done any plumbing inside at all. How does he know that I didn't just cut the skin, get bored, sew up and go home?

Every time I hear experts talking on the television or radio I get the twitches. Streams of dogma pour out of their mouths and because they are experts the so-called facts are taken as truths. It is so easy to present facts these days. We live in an age of blind acceptance of the word of experts. No one ever challenges the source of the facts. What do they base their arguments on, how was the data collected, who collected it, is he reliable? Have the results been ever so slightly bent? Oh, and the fun you can have with percentages . . . There was a percentage change of so much, so many per cent of people do this or that, there is a so many per cent advantage in one course of action. They all sound very impressive until you relate them to the absolute number involved, and then they often become meaningless.

Today there are experts in everything and they all pour out statements that we are expected to accept. As from today, don't. Discover the word 'why'. Pursue a policy of conditional acceptance. . . OK, you may be right in what you say but first tell me why. Who are you? What are your credentials? How do I know that what you say is true? I'm not saying that you shouldn't trust people but you should certainly make them earn your trust. Trust should be one of your most precious possessions. Never give it away free. Make sure that whoever receives it from you knows how to look after it. Don't squander it.

And that brings me back to my own job. Surgeons are only technicians doing a job. If you find yourself in hospital needing an operation please ask why. It's your body after all and you've a right to know what's going on. The days of mysticism and magic in medicine are fast disappearing. If your doctor won't tell you why, don't trust him. He's not worth it. By the way, if he says, 'Well actually I haven't a clue what is wrong with you but I've several ideas for finding out,' this is one of the best things you can hear because it means he is honest. Make sure he earns your trust. Don't be overawed by his pompous manner. You can get immense fun out of deflating pompous men by challenging what they say. That's quite a point actually; asking why not only satisfies your curiosity it can also give you a great deal of fun. Chuck out blind acceptance. Don't be trodden on by the experts. Stir up the world a bit and enjoy yourself with one little word – 'Why?'

2. LESLIE BREWER

To know you have been efficient enough to have bought fuse-wire; and, what's more, to remember where you have put it, takes quite a lot of the sting out of a sudden domestic black-out; particularly if you have been efficient enough to have a torch, too, where you can lay your hand on it immediately.

The trouble with all real efficiency is that other people don't notice it. They only notice its absence. It is taken for granted that you put that apple in the school satchel every night to save panic and waste of precious time in the morning before a child gets off to school. Nothing's ever said . . . until that morning when your efficiency, for some reason, breaks down and there's no apple.

We, at school, know when home is not being very efficient, when three sisters turn up with one school-hat between them. And a parent grumbles when a headmaster, who should know her, obviously doesn't know her from Mrs Adam. No praise for the hundred other faces rightly named and children remembered.

I've always enjoyed the story of the headmaster (no doubt very efficient) who suddenly had a lapse one Old Boys' Day. He pumped a middle-aged man's hand up and down and said heartily, 'Now let me see, was it you or your brother who was killed in the War?'

But, seriously, where children are concerned, it's a pity if there are too many lapses. And, also, too much obvious efficiency. I see efficiency, in school or at home, as an invisible, all-supporting framework to children's lives, like the strong forgotten beams of wood in a house.

We're efficient for the children's sake. Not for efficiency's sake, not even for the private pleasure of always having clean clothes ready just when they're needed, breakfast ready on the dot. And, at the same time – and I think this is all-important – we're not unduly upset, ourselves, when our efficiency breaks down, lapses occasionally. A child shouldn't be utterly thrown – it shouldn't be a matter of tears or temper, when, for once, that apple hasn't been put in the satchel the night before.

All schools know the young child who is badly put out by any change in routine, change caused by, yes, inefficiency, or sometimes, just a belief that a bit of change, occasionally, is good for us all. He or she, almost certainly, comes from a home where mother is equally upset, or guilty, or over-anxious, when a sacred routine is departed from.

I believe that if possible we should get (and young children get) a sense of security – not guilt, nor anxiety, from efficiency. Anxiety only happens when we put efficiency for its own sake above people. I think if there is real security there'll be laughter, not tears and tantrums, when mum has an occasional lapse.

Today there are young parents who are almost afraid of efficiency, of having routines, because efficiency asks – demands, if you like – something from others, even children, if it is to work. And they jib at making any demands. By a false logic the argument goes if you are not efficient, you don't need to ask anything from your children. And that's supposed, by some, to be a good thing. So be shambolic, almost on principle! There are schools today, too, for young children where there is no set routine, where no demands are made. I doubt whether children are very happy, or very secure, under such conditions. It is usually rather a false 'freedom'. You may not have breakfast on the dot but something's got to be eaten before school; after all, it is breakfast time. And the school, however free and easy, demands that the children turn up at nine. They're just different demands.

Should we demand, 'expect' if you like, efficiency from our children? I think so. I do, in school. And with children as young as six or seven. They can have the right book ready at the right time, know just where their Wellington boots are, take small but real responsibilities.

Unfortunately, the too-efficient mothers sometimes take away this legitimate pleasure from small children, and miss a chance to encourage them to be efficient and shed a bit of Mother's load. Some mums want to see, in the morning, that the Wellingtons are tidily placed so that they can easily be found at break. They see the homework (as well as the apple) is in that satchel. The poor child isn't given a chance. It's too sheltered from the consequences of its own un-tidiness, forgetfulness – it's own inefficiency. And we all, old or young, only become efficient by realising how uncomfortable, how wasteful of time, temper and spirit, it is, not to be reasonably efficient.

3. JOHN CASSON

'When you want to kick a man downstairs,' said G. K. Chesterton, 'you don't worry about which are the correct muscles to use, or how much force you are going to apply with them. You only think of the beatific picture of the fellow in a heap at the bottom of the stairs with yourself standing triumphantly at the top.' This quotation may not be entirely accurate but I think I have got the gist of it. Men of action, Chesterton believed, don't talk about doing things. They are far too busy doing them. On the whole it is only the sick people who talk about their health. Healthy people have something better to do with their time. They have things to do. It is the same with most of the talk about efficiency. People talk about it when they are not performing well, when they are not very efficient.

But it seems to me that the word efficiency is really only a kind of shorthand symbol to indicate all those things that are done well and achieve their object.

I never think it particularly efficient to drive along a splendidly constructed highway for a hundred miles in a superbly designed car just to play pin-ball at the other end, nor to make enormous profits in a business simply to be able to show a sound balance sheet to anyone who might care to look at it. I met a chief accountant the other day who vetoed a much-needed reorganisation of a factory because it would upset their system of accounting! It was a most efficient system for describing and accounting for a most inefficient manufacturing process. Accounts are only descriptions of things, not the things themselves.

We don't want to be like the lunatic who at lunch-time writes the words 'steak and onions' on a piece of paper and then eats the paper. In his view he has eaten steak and onions – the words and the objects are to him identical, and as long as he has got hold of the right words he is convinced that he's had a good meal by them. Words are like maps that help us more effectively to use and organise the territory of the world we live in. But it is the territory that matters, not the map, not the words. You can't increase the profits of a company by going to lectures about efficiency, but only by having a look at a number of operations and working out how to perform them more efficiently, that is by improving the territory rather than by drawing a better map.

Many years ago my father, Lewis Casson, was asked to open a new school for actors. After the ceremony he spoke to the pupils. 'I wonder how many of you,' he asked in a gentle, kindly voice, 'have come to this school because you

want to *be* great actors.' There was much preening and
giggling by the pupils who clearly had this aim in mind.
'Because if there are any of you with that idea,' he went on
in the same friendly voice, 'I can only say to you that the
sooner you get out of this profession the better for all
concerned. But if you are determined to use what gifts you
have and to work very hard at improving them in order to
do something worthwhile in return for the food, clothing,
shelter and luxuries that the rest of the community will give
you, then you'll be so busy that you won't have time to
worry about *being* something. But you will then much more
probably *be* something worthwhile.'

4. JOYCE GRENFELL

Order means light and peace, inward liberty and free
command over oneself; order is power. . . order is man's
great need and his true well-being. (Denis Amiel.)

It's odd the way it has become a criticism to say anyone
is 'efficient'. It suggests that something important is missing.
You read it in notices about actors, painters, writers,
musicians, and you hear it about individuals: 'He's very
efficient. . .' meaning he functions like a machine but
doesn't add a special quality of his own. I don't accept this
use of the word because I believe what Webster says about it
in his dictionary: 'Efficient: Immediately effective. Highly
capable and *productive*.'

I see efficiency as a kind of oil for making wheels turn
more smoothly. It's a talent on its own and a fulfilment and
it can be enjoyed by anyone who wants it. Anyone. It
doesn't just happen, it has to be worked for and, when it
has arrived at the 'highly productive' product, is harmon-
ious activity in whatever job, calling or endeavour it is put

to, whether it is in an office, factory, studio, shop, playing field or home. Efficiency makes things work better, not only for the one who has it but for all who come into contact with him – or her!

Take punctuality. Sometimes unpunctuality is worn with a kind of pride: 'Sorry, I'm afraid I'm always late.' This is a form of self-centred arrogance. It lacks caring about other people and their time. It's inefficient and un-productive of anything except irritation.

I get enormous satisfaction and pleasure, watching anyone do almost anything very well. Not only obvious things like dancing, juggling, playing the piano and tennis; but little jobs like potting a seedling, darning a great gape of a hole in a sock, bathing a baby, folding in white of egg (so difficult I find), building a wall, polishing silver and shoes. What I like about this sort of efficiency is the confident attack and rhythm with which people who know how to do a job do it with the freedom of skill. And it comes about through caring enough to learn the right way – or inventing a new way – and then practising it, through experience, to realisation. Maybe you do have to have a special talent for lace-making, opera and kicking a football but anyone who cares enough can learn to achieve order in what they are called upon to do and this comes by way of efficiency.

I am not tidy at my desk, my stocking drawer . . . don't let's think about it. I wish I knew how to keep shoes under control in a cupboard even with racks. But I do love and need order in my life and I'm learning that it comes by getting priorities right. First things first.

I think the story of Mary and Martha is a pointer. There was Martha 'cumbered about with much serving' and feeling hard done by, while Mary is sitting quietly learning from Jesus's teaching. Martha is incensed by this and says, in the New English Bible version, 'Lord, do you not care that my sister has left me to get on with the work by myself? Tell her to come and lend a hand.' But the Lord answered, 'Martha, Martha, you are fretting and fussing about so many things; but one thing is necessary. The part Mary has chosen is best; and it shall not be taken away from her.'

I have a feeling Jesus had said these things to Martha before because he uses her name twice, as you do when you are going over something *again*! I think he is saying, Martha, Martha, get your priorities right. First things first. Seek ye first the Kingdom of Heaven and then all the rest will be added unto you – such as order, peace of mind, fulfilment, efficiency.

For me, efficiency is more than not running out of butter, typewriter ribbons and time. It is surely caring in its highest meaning, putting first things first, and that is love.

5. PETER WYLD

I read an article a few weeks ago about the blood transfusion service in different countries. It was very interesting because it demonstrated fairly forcibly that the most efficient service in the world is the one we have here, where people give their blood free. Our transfusion service is not the most highly organised but it is about the most human, and that works out at being the most efficient. Efficiency isn't just a question of smooth organisation.

Of course you want to make a good job of everything you do. You probably know those awful house-proud women who always have everything in its place and clean and neat and perfect in their houses – perfect that is as regards hygiene and tidiness but an absolute washout as a home. Hopelessly inefficient as a place for children to be free in, to play and grow up in. Useless as a place to make strangers feel welcome, dismal for a man to come back to from work. No fun because the housewife forgot that a house exists not for tidiness, but for being human in. She is very inefficient at human living, that woman. Human living is what homes and families are for; efficiency means everything that helps living to be human, and inefficiency means everything that stops it being. There is great pleasure always in good work done and good workmanship. For instance there must be pleasure for the people who make all those clever little hydrogen bombs. Very efficient they are at making fancy bombs, but the whole job seems a pretty clumsy way of keeping the peace between the great powers, and very dangerous. Inefficient in fact, though apparently the best we can do at present. You have to ask what things are efficient *for*.

Let us go one step further and see if we can see what an efficient human is, by asking what human living is for. If I could get all your answers together it's a fair certainty that most of them would contain words like happiness and peace and security and enjoyment and friendship and love – and also words like help and kindness and service and consideration.

And if you're a Christian you might sum it up in one word, because Christians have a very loud one-word answer to what human living is for and this is a good day to think of it. Glory. And the reason it is a good day to think of it is because today is Ascension Day. About Jesus ascending into heaven, and man beginning to share the life of God and the glory of God.

My boss in the office told me a marvellous thing the other day. He hadn't thought of it himself – it was first said by St Ireneaus who was a bishop in France about eighteen hundred years ago. 'The glory of God is man fully alive.'

Oh, do think about that. Fully alive, that's glory. That's what human living is for, that's what you and I were made for. That's why Jesus ascended into heaven. So that man can be fully alive.

Of course there are lots of things that get in the way of glory – everything from toothache to prejudice, everything from hatred to exhaustion, everything from bronchitis to revenge. Man does not usually manage to glorify God by being fully alive – there are a hundred different things that prevent him. But that is the inefficiency of the world. You and I fail to be human – sometimes through our own fault, sometimes through others' fault, sometimes through no one's, but just because the world *is* cockeyed (what's called original sin – the built-in bentness that you can't dodge). It is a pretty inefficient world with lots of things standing in the way of man fully alive.

And our business is to remove these obstacles to glory, the things that prevent full life. We're awfully good at stopping people dying nowadays, but we are only at the start of helping them to live. All over the world not enough protein to make good brains and bodies, not enough education to make good minds capable of enjoying good things, not enough love to make man fully alive.

It's good that Christian Aid Week and Ascension Day should overlap this year because they are both about the same thing; about life for man. Keep longing for glory, keep caring that man should be fully alive. Help to make people human and free and efficient.

6. A COUNTRY DOCTOR

No doubt the word 'efficiency' when applied to the Health Service conjures up visions not only of ample hospital beds, ambulances, wonder drugs and free everything, but also of laboratories, vast operating theatres, bigger and better X-rays and electrical diagnostic gadgetry; inferring at least the possibility of complete scientific control of our bodies and the state-assisted ability not only to overcome all disease but to protect us from all forms of suffering. Only a short step to feeding symptoms into a computer which will then prescribe an infallible treatment.

But I still find that people as a whole cherish the concept of their family doctor as a friend and counsellor, sympathetically involved in their problems and understanding them as 'human beings'.

Yet in this technological age the multiplicity of diagnostic tests a patient may be subjected to, the variety of departments in a hospital he may pass through, the large armoury of drugs available, acting not only on the body but also on the personality – all these have induced in us the idea that there must be a specific cure for every ailment any one individual may contract; and that it is the duty of the efficient doctor to find it.

I think it is we doctors, dazzled by the amazing increase in scientific aids to diagnosis and treatment, who are responsible for the widespread forgetfulness of one fundamental fact – the practitioner of medicine hardly ever *himself* heals anyone: the power of healing is within the patient, the efficient doctor merely assists in a natural process.

At my medical school, the Chair of Public Health and Hygiene was held by Professor Auden, father of the poet; and he had a dictum we should all remember, 'Healing is not a science, it is the intuitive wooing of Nature.'

We do so easily forget that we are part of 'nature'. Like animals and plants we have within us a life-force, the same life-force: if we cut ourselves, the wound will heal itself, sooner or later, whether a doctor stitches and dresses it or not. And certainly *he* couldn't make it heal; if we are invaded by germs and get pneumonia the body immediately produces agents to kill those germs; when we are desperately ill the body continues to fight for survival even if we are unconscious, even if we claim to be 'tired of life'.

Again, most illness is due to fighting against nature. As we poison the rest of creation with plastic waste, oil-slicks, poisonous gases and pesticides, so we poison ourselves too – not only by immoderate consumption of tobacco, alcohol and food; but also by leading unnatural lives. Our highly industrialised competitive society subjects young executives to strains they were not made to withstand and condemns thousands to repetitive, meaningless and unsatisfying work. In both cases, physical disease so often is the symptom of the underlying tension. And our urban society deprives most of us from absorbing the age-old healing wisdom of the natural world, while providing endless distractions, hiding from us the cause of our malaise.

This is not a 'back to nature' cry, but an attempt to show that most illness is the result of lack of adjustment between the body and its environment. It follows that an efficient doctor, while helping his patient to come to terms with his more general environment, should seek to place him in the best possible immediate environment for natural healing to take place. That may involve antibiotics to help the system overcome infection, analgesics to ease pain, sedatives to encourage sleep and so on. But it also involves trying to understand the person involved, his work and his home; remembering that no two individuals are ever exactly alike.

Sharing Experience

1. A Sense of Discovery
JOYCE GRENFELL

If I were asked what I thought life is for I'd say it is for making discoveries; and I think the greatest gift anyone can have is an unending sense of discovery, and with it an increasing awareness of delight and wonder.

The kind of discovery I mean comes on many levels. As a child you begin by discovering your fingers and toes; you discover walking and talking and singing and laughing. But before this comes trust. Trust is evidently instinctive and I suspect the reason for this is that trust is love and love is an everlasting value that is always there to be found. In fact everything worth discovering is already in existence.

We may lose sight of love. We may meet with straight denials of it – cruelty, for instance, is a pretty rough rebuff to love – but nevertheless Love as a power and as a continuing energy is ever present and we are all spiritually endowed to find it. It may take real hunger for it and much practice to find it, but a sense of discovery of love is the spiritual awareness we can all discover, experience and use.

There's a big difference between nosey-parker curiosity and the sense of discovery I mean. This seeks to know what is to be trusted – what is good – what lasts; only that which is dependable, practical and forever is good.

I've always had an instinctive feeling and belief in love as a real power – I was told this by my parents but proofs down the years have made it my own and a few years ago I had an experience which is still a reminder of this power.

I landed from a ship on a bitterly cold, dark January day very early in the morning and I stood in a vile wind in the exposed customs shed surrounded by eleven pieces of luggage. I was on a concert tour. I had microphone equipment, stage dresses, make-up case etc. The customs man appeared, huge and furious, with his coat collar turned up and his head down. He was in a brutal mood, sullen and surly and bullying.

'Open your bags,' he said.

I said, 'Which one?'

'*I said open your bags* – all of them!'

My brother and a friend who had come to meet me were about to get into the situation. I saw the ominous tightening of my brother's upper lip! So I put my hand on his arm and heard myself say, 'No don't – we'll love him out of it.' Not at first glance a very appropriate thing to say. I really hardly knew what I meant by it but I had suddenly seen that here was a man with a large lump of seething resentment that he needed to get rid of and the nearest chest on to which he could dump it was mine! If I refused to accept the load of resentment it would have nowhere to go. It must fall to the ground. I refused to accept it.

The discovery was that – whether he realised it or not – he did need to get rid of the resentment because in fact it was no part of his true self – the self that is spiritually the likeness of his Creator, God.

'OK,' I said and I got out all the keys and bent down and opened up every one of those bags. There was complete silence. The customs man made a very token sort of examination of one bag and then bent down to help me refasten them all. He said something about it was a rule that all the bags must be opened. He became gentle, friendly, even pleasant! Whatever it was that had been burning him up had fallen to the ground and burnt itself out. He said he hoped

I'd enjoy visiting his country. We parted with smiles.

I was as surprised as my brother at the complete change of attitude. The discovery that love has its own power was one of the most moving and useful I have ever made. Of course the fact was always there to be discovered. All good things are.

2. By-products

MARGARET BENTLEY

It was one of those days when you start late and everything goes wrong. I hurried through the jobs thinking 'I *must* get the shopping done before lunch.' In a fever of impatience I pulled on my coat and slammed the door. Half an hour later I was back with a bulging shopping-bag, groping for my key. Oh, no! I must have left it in another coat. The last straw, stuck on the doorstep, locked out, with a hundred jobs waiting inside.

I prowled round the house – not *one* open window. I sat on the doorstep and scowled at the garden. Then inspiration. I could telephone my husband. He'd come home and let me in.

I set off along the road. Past the next-door house, and the next. For some inexplicable reason, I decided to ask a widow I hardly knew if I could use her telephone. She looked pale, and there were dark shadows under her eyes. Quickly I made my telephone call. We stood again in the quiet kitchen – me bustling and urgent, and she silent with her loss.

'I'm sorry you had to find me on one of my bad days,' she said.

Her quiet dignity told me more than any words. I knew, just a fraction, of what the last year had meant to her. And I thought of all the things I didn't know how to say. For one clear as crystal second we saw into each other's minds.

I went home calm and changed. The day was altered in a fundamental and timeless fashion. I'd lost an hour and gained just a little in understanding.

Another time I was rushing home after a meeting, tired after a poor night's sleep, late again, everything to do.

'I'll give you a lift,' said a friend. Good, that would save a few minutes waiting for a bus.

Half-way home, her car stalled on a hill. The gears jammed. Nothing she could do seemed to help. Time was speeding by. And we looked like being here for ages. My friend set off to walk to a garage. I'd be later than ever now. Then I remembered a book I'd bought on impulse that very morning – poetry, beautifully illustrated. I read it from cover to cover and as the quiet words filled my mind a sense of peace stole over me. It was years since I had sat reading poetry. I was almost sorry when my friend came back.

It's strange how these by-products, these unexpected bonuses, become the things you remember with pleasure, and sometimes gratitude. I accept that 'No man is an island', but that doesn't stop me sometimes trying to be an island – on my own. I remember the time after my daughter was born. They were trundling me through the hospital corridors on a trolley and I almost prayed, 'Oh, let them put me in a room on my own.' But on we went – past the cubicles to the ward at the end. Five other women as well as me. I thought I'd hate it, but I didn't. I learned about their hopes and their fears, and in doing so, my own worries and minor discomforts fell into proportion.

Our children are teenagers now, and family outings are fewer. My husband decided to have a day off so that we could all go to the coast. The morning came; mild rebellion in the house – our son didn't want to go, neither did our daughter. I think that was the day we realised family life is an ever-changing pattern. It was too late for the outing now. 'Come on,' I said to my husband. 'Let's you and I go for a walk on the moors.'

We set off – the two of us. We'd almost got out of the habit of a long walk together. Now we're planning a walking holiday next year. When I think of the things I've cried over that have been blessings in disguise, I know I'd be a fool if I *didn't* live in hope.

3. Widening Horizons
TOM HETHERINGTON

A few weeks ago, our daughter, like thousands of other youngsters, packed her bags and left home to go to college. It's a natural progression of events: you push them into their first school as toddlers, you notice the change when they go to some form of secondary school, and then suddenly it's over and they've departed for college or an employment.

And you know that's how it has got to be – they'd go sour on you if they couldn't move forward and embrace new horizons. It's the going forward that counts: the invigorating freshness of new experience. The trouble is, I've found as I've got older that there comes a point in time when the youthful desire for fresh experience is counterbalanced by the lazy comfort of accepted routine. And from then on, the battle is joined (or at least it is if you have any primitive impulse to stay alive and be master of your own destiny) not to become an unthinking vegetable before you're forty. It is the forces of inertia against the forces of sprightly-mindedness, and the battle-line will sway backwards and forwards – at least, it does in my case.

Perhaps I should have called them 'expanding frontiers' rather than 'widening horizons', but whether I'm expanding or widening, I know I feel immensely pleased with myself if a burst of energy puts me on the winning side for a while. Certainly there's no standing still in this struggle: you advance, or you begin to retreat. My job is teacher-training. I spend a lot of time giving advisory interviews to older people thinking of taking up teaching as a career. It bothers me sometimes when one of them says he 'finished' his education twelve years ago – and really sounds as though he means it.

I think none of us finished our education twelve years ago – or two years ago. It's never finished. The materials for further education are there all the time, and it doesn't have to be in a classroom or lecture room, though there's plenty of that too. There's never been better provision of courses for every subject and interest under the sun than there is today, in evening institutes and technical colleges, just to take one field of activity. If you want to navigate a boat, breed tropical fish, or dismember your car to its uttermost parts, there's someone standing by ready to tell you how to do it. If you're lucky enough to be going abroad next summer, the radio or the tv will instruct you in enough of the language of the country to get you started.

After a year's tv German lessons, I doubt whether I'm as good as many viewers who took the course, as I wasn't able to give much time to it. But when we visited Austria this summer, I did at least manage to use the language in shops and restaurants, and for retrieving ourselves when we got lost. In a very small way, I felt I was making direct contact with the people of another country, instead of being encapsuled in English. That's the important thing – and the fact that it whetted my appetite for more. Perhaps that all sounds a bit boastful. I don't feel boastful about another situation, and this was much nearer home.

An old man was approaching me in the road. His appearance was ragged, but not nearly so ragged as the music he was producing from a violin. It was a dreadful sound. 'Oh, grief,' I thought, 'not another of them!' And I kept my eyes firmly fixed in front of me and prepared to pass by literally on the other side.

At this moment, a front door opened, and a hippy-looking youth came out – bearded, jeans, and the rest. I'd often eyed him with disfavour. He walked straight down the garden path and over to the old man. 'That's the stuff, grand-dad,' he said. 'That's great, great. Nothing like a bit o' music, is there?' And there was the tinkle of coins in the old man's box.

I felt mortally ashamed of myself. I went across the road and added my contribution, but it wasn't the same, and I knew it wasn't. The only comfort I can extract from this brief happening is that the lesson was good for me. It was certainly just as much a lesson as anything I did in German. Not all education after school need be formal instruction. I've found there's a great deal you can pick up as you're going along. But you can't see widening horizons if you keep your eyes and your mind tight shut. You only benefit from your experience if you're aware it's happening – and if you're always prepared to learn from it.

I've decided in the last few years that this is one of the principal dangers I'll have to watch. It becomes very easy to opt out, let the world pass by. I ask myself: how long is it since I last took a good close look at a butterfly? or a man opposite me in a train? or really listened to what a colleague has to say about the problems in her department?

If I let these things go, take people and situations for granted, then my horizons won't get wider. They'll come closer, get narrower. My world will get smaller and my view more restricted. And that worries me. Because I don't want to live in a smaller world.

4. Unselfishness

VICTOR RIPLEY

There's a man on my train to work every day who opens the window and then takes care to sit where the cold air doesn't touch him. It's a small annoyance, no more than that, but it's a daily reminder of something that has been occupying my thoughts more and more over the past few years. As I see it, the fundamental difference between people is how they stand on the scale of selfishness; how close to themselves their interests lie.

My fellow commuter wants his fresh air but would rather someone else paid the price of being buffeted by the wind. In other words, he's more concerned with his own comfort than with that of another person. Now, take that indifference to others' comfort to an extreme and you have someone who will, perhaps, strike out to get his own way; you have a hit-and-run driver so insulated against his victim's sufferings that he will not stop; you have, at the very end of the scale, the ultimate selfishness of the murderer. Of course, the man at the train window isn't going to end up killing the whole carriage load one morning – at least, I hope he's not. I'm not suggesting that he's on some doom-laden course that will take him inexorably into violence. But he's exhibiting in a small and easily recognised way the defect that blights all our human contacts. We all do things that we know will distress others because our well-being matters more than theirs.

Some days ago, I was hurrying to catch a bus in Fleet Street when I noticed a man, white stick in hand, standing by the kerb, willing some passer-by to guide him across the road. If I had stayed and missed the bus, it wouldn't have mattered too much; anyway, there were a lot of people about, and one of them would surely go to his aid. So I caught my bus and sat in silent contempt for myself throughout the journey. I had cared, but I hadn't cared enough at that moment to overcome my own self-concern. This was real selfishness, what my dictionary calls, 'void of regard for others'. And I believe that it's to be found at the bottom of all our troubles – personal, domestic, social, industrial, national, international affairs. The inability, or unwillingness, to try to feel what others feel, which will turn a family disagreement into a bitter division, is the same as that which makes a shop-floor grievance into a strike or a border dispute into a war between states. Selfishness is the one common crime by humanity against humanity because it is the foundation on which all others are built.

Because it's so fundamental, it's also the hardest to challenge successfully. Two thousand years of 'Love thy neighbour as thyself' have hardly touched it, and I certainly don't pretend to offer any instant solution. All I can do is hope to win my personal battles against my own self-interest, and try to demonstrate to my children that others' feelings count as much as theirs.

There's a little book by Maurice Sendak which both of them have loved, about a boy called Pierre who takes it into his head one day to cut himself off from his family by refusing to get involved. No matter what his parents say to him his response is, 'I don't care'. He ends up, having been eaten by a lion and then rescued alive, by agreeing that maybe it is better to take account of what other people say and do. Sendak ends his tale with six words, 'The moral of Pierre is: care.'

It's very nearly a complete philosophy of life. The only change I would make would be to add one more word. Care *enough*.

Grace and Good Manners

I. ARTHUR HELLIWELL

In these days of crumbling standards and tarnished values just how important do you think good manners are? Are they, perhaps, an outmoded luxury in an 'I'm all right Jack' society? Are the conventional little everyday courtesies that people of my generation were taught, as we grew up, to regard as essential, really necessary any longer? Does it really matter if we don't say 'Please' and 'Thank you' and 'I beg your pardon' any more? Or hold open doors? Or give up our seats in buses and trains?

Well, I think it does. I'm sufficiently old-fashioned to believe that good manners *are* important. In fact very important. And I am equally convinced that the decline in polite behaviour has a lot to do with the spread of violence, tension and lack of understanding. Now we blame the rat race for this. But just how much are we ourselves to blame for the rat race? Without this infernal desire to 'Keep up with the Joneses' in a world that has gone madly materialistic there would be no rat race. And we should all be a lot better mannered. America – or I should say New York, because it's unfair to judge a whole nation by the behaviour of one city – New York is a perfect and frightening example of the point I am trying to make. The richest city in the world, inhabited by the rudest people in the world. A concrete jungle of unparalleled affluence and unequalled violence. The poor New Yorkers are all so busy chasing a living that they have no time for good manners. And the impact of this pushing, shoving, snapping, snarling society on the visitor is as startling as encountering a tribe of howling savages in the Congo jungle. I know. I have lived in both places. And I prefer the African jungle to Broadway or Fifth Avenue.

When we lived in New York I travelled to my office by bus along Third Avenue, and one morning soon after we arrived I struggled to my feet to offer my seat to a woman on the crowded single-decker. At first she ignored me, but when I raised my hat and said, 'Please take my seat madam,' she backed away in real alarm. 'Hey Mac,' she shouted. 'What's the big idea? You some kind of a sex nut or sump'n?' By this time the whole bus was staring and muttering, so, blushing furiously, I jumped off at the next stop and walked to work.

The trouble is that this kind of behaviour is infectious. I never again offered a seat to anyone on a New York bus, and at the end of our first year there I was as ruthlessly uncouth as the rest of them. You had to be to survive. 'Excuse me please' won't get you anywhere in Manhattan. If you're at the rear of a crowded lift you brusquely announce, 'Gittin' out' – and shove. 'I beg your pardon' is an equal waste of time. And when no one says 'thank-you' you soon forget to say 'please'.

I have travelled six times around the world. And one curious thing you notice when you do this is that manners gradually improve as you travel East, until you reach the Orient where courtesy and politeness are refined to a point of quite exquisite delicacy. I once dined with a Chinese millionaire whose wife and daughters – all cultured and intelligent women – stood behind our chairs throughout the meal anticipating our every need. Frankly I found this embarrassing. And of course there's no place for such behaviour in emancipated Western society. But surely somewhere there must be a happy mean between East and West.

2. R. D. SMITH

We all know the times they are a-changing and it's natural that the way we use and react to words is changing too. 'Grace and good manners' once were the OK-est of words, as the things they described were the most respected of states. But today I suspect a good many people think that we established hacks use the words to describe sissy, or old-fashioned, or snobbish, behaviour.

And I believe the ear-bashing that goes on in the mass media, which means the huge advertising organisations, angled to push us into new popular ways of 'living with spending', obscures a stubborn fact: there are still places and people that have not been changed or corrupted by the greed for money and prestige: there are still people who think that what journalists call abrasive and tough behaviour is ugly behaviour, whatever the politicians and tv careerists say; as in New Zealand and South African rugby football, what they call 'hard play' is often in fact dirty play.

There are still people who prefer co-operation to competition, beauty and peace to commercial development and concrete progress, grace to ruthless efficiency, good manners to the neurotic aggression of the social pecking order. More respect for grace and good manners would mean less psychiatry and millions fewer buck-you-up and send-you-to sleep pellets and pills.

Now grace is one thing and good manners another: but they have in common their effortlessness; an ease and a beauty that comes from unawareness of self. In theological terms grace is the unmerited love and favour of God in Christ, or salvation freely provided. There was no wheeler-dealering there. So grace was a gift, not won by competition. And in life it still expresses something given, not striven for; a child sleeping, a cat stretching, Georgie Best gliding through, not the lout who chops and hacks him, Lloyd fielding for Lancashire, Graveney off-driving, Barry John or Cantoni swerving through a broken field, Mohammed Ali feinting and floating, wind in a field of wheat, swans on water, geese flying. No repetition or vulgarisation can destroy these moments of action that come very near to poetry or music.

They are moments that will and purpose and effort and training alone can never attain to. Similarly, good manners are not things you wrestle for and with, they are not the social behaviour patterns of a superior social class as the handbooks on keeping up with the Joneses and all the U and non-U racket rather damnably imply. I say 'damnably' because they suggest that words and manners are weapons for social struggle or tools for social climbing. And I believe a great many insecure people have been made even more insecure by being told that what comes naturally to them is something that is, in a social sense, inferior.

Good manners are ways of behaving in which you lose yourself for a while in consideration and care for someone else. The phrase 'one of nature's gentlemen' is not an archaic or an empty one. It recalls 'When Adam digged and Eve span, who was then the gentleman?' But it also recognises that good manners have not to do with the clothing and fashions and actions of the upper classes, but with acceptance of the great truth that we are members one of another ... Good manners consist in doing as you would be done by. That's why some brusque people may not be conceived as having bad manners if they behave consistently to everyone.

I don't believe all is lost. Many people loathe the rat race: tens of thousands of young people have turned away from it. And as MacNeice says:

'Man is a spirit and symbols are his meat,

So pull not down your steeple in your monied street.'

3. PAUL CHEETHAM

I remember being surprised, on my first visit to Spain, by the fact that the Spaniards, noted for their good manners, rarely say 'please, and 'thank you'.

In our country, too, there are differences between north and south. Northerners generally find the gushing enthusiasm over what *they* see as trifles embarrassing and unnecessary, while southerners tend to be offended by the apparent coolness with which northerners receive presents or hospitality.

The times, too, are rapidly changing, and what was regarded as outrageous in dress, manners or morals ten years ago is now generally accepted. In the words of the song, 'Anything goes'. There are those who threw up their hands in horror at this development and who look back longingly to the vanished manners and conventions which characterised what they regard as a civilised society. It is tempting, but often not very honest, to be nostalgic. If we look at history, we find that groups of people, noted for their good manners in society, could, and very often did, behave brutally towards those they regarded as inferiors. For example, only a hundred years ago the aristocracy and middle classes of Victorian England treated the working classes like slaves. Certainly these slaves were polite and respectful to their masters, but only because their lives and jobs depended on it.

This brings us to what I consider to be the essentials of good manners. It is the habit of considering the needs of other people, of putting their interests before your own. If we stick to this idea, although our behaviour may vary among different groups of people, it will still be good manners. It is this sort of consideration which leads young men to give up their seats in trains and buses, motorists to drive slowly past schools and playgrounds, and all of us to anticipate the needs of the elderly. We would all agree about this, but there are more controversial matters. For example, I think it is true to say that many schoolmasters like to be addressed as 'Sir'. It is flattering and gives one a sense of power, or at least of superiority. But surely it is only good manners if it meets the needs of the master concerned. Boys can call you 'Sir' and still be extremely rude. What I find irritating in class is interruption, whether of myself or of anyone else who is speaking. This I regard as bad manners, if it arises not because someone cannot understand what is being said, but because he wants to draw attention to himself, hold up the class or stop others getting a word in edgeways. It is sometimes said that girls have better manners than boys, because they are naturally less aggressive and boisterous, but I think it is just as ill-mannered for girls to giggle and polish their nails at the back of the class as for a crowd of boys to push and jostle others through a doorway.

Schoolmasters and parents are often worried about what manners to teach their children. Rather than set rules which may not apply in ten years' time, perhaps the best thing would be to teach them to ask themselves first the question, 'What does this person need?' We don't interrupt other people because they have a right to be heard. We give up our seats to those who are weaker than ourselves. We take special care to express our gratitude to people to whom we know this matters. We pay various courtesies to those for whom we know these courtesies are important. It is this consideration, I think, which the poet Spenser had in mind when he wrote:

'The gentle mind by gentle deeds is known.
For a man by nothing is so well betray'd
As by his manners.'

4. THE BISHOP OF LIVERPOOL

There are some words we use which time and usage have not spoiled. Take the word 'graceful', for example – we apply it to the flowing movements of a ballerina, of a tennis player, of a swimmer. And, very differently, we speak of the graceful lines of a car, of a ship, of an aeroplane. Recently, for the first time in my life, I was taken on board a large racing yacht. It was heavenly weather, the sea was blue, the wind moderate. I was vividly aware of grace – the grace of the helmsman, measuring his distances and angles to a nicety, the grace of the sails as they swung into position, the grace of smooth, noiseless movement, the grace of human beings at leisure from themselves and at peace with each other.

I suppose 'graceful' – having grace – suggests ease. No apparent effort. But of course, we know that behind the graceful movement of the ballerina, behind the smooth movement of a yacht, there lies a whole world of training and discipline and – yes – effort too. There's a co-ordination of muscle, economy of energy and an exact adjustment of movement and rhythm. And the impression is of effortless mastery. Contrast the poor amateur – floundering, struggling, expending vast quantities of energy – and all to negligible effect.

It was once said of Jesus of Nazareth that he was 'full of grace'. And I think this simply means that those who knew him best could see in his life – a style if you like – that also belongs to the prima ballerina or the first-rate yachtsman. I mean he gave to his friends the impression of effortless mastery over the conditions of human life. It was an arduous, costly, rigorous life that he lived, as the records show – constantly harried by crowds, pursued by his enemies, misunderstood by his friends and finally subjected to torture of body, mind and spirit. And all that to a degree which few of us could begin to imagine. Yet inwardly he appeared to be at rest, confident, poised, assured, drawing on unfailing spiritual resources as out of a deep well. He was at home in the universe.

What was the secret of this extraordinary, graceful life? Well he himself would have said, *did* say, that he owed all his invincible confidence to the One he spoke of as his heavenly Father, creator of the universe, lover of mankind.

It was his joy, he said, to do his Father's will, and by so doing he drew upon all the mighty resources of the One who'd made the heavens and the earth. The spiritual riches of the universe were at his disposal, not for his own selfish use, but for the blessing and healing of his friends. He lived by grace, he was 'full of grace'.

And here are we, stumbling over our partner's feet, rushing round the court trying to keep the ball in play, tangled up in the lines and in danger of falling overboard. In fact, banging about in the universe like bulls in a china shop – a picture, all too often, of graceless, clumsy effort that leaves us spent to no effect.

Kenneth Fearing's zany verse describes it well:

'And wow he died, as wow he lived,

Going whop to the office, and blowie home to sleep and biff got married and bam had children and oof got fired.

Zowie did he live and zowie did he die.

But, thank God, there is a more constructive, more graceful way of living than that. And it's a way that's possible for anyone willing to face the claims of Jesus Christ. If his promises are true – and I'm sure they are – the style of his life can be the style of ours. His grace, the Bible says, is sufficient for us, however unhappy and desperate our circumstances may be. St Paul knew a thing or two when he prayed that the grace of our Lord Jesus Christ should be with us all. And who would deny that we need that grace, if life is to be what God intends it to be.

Christmas

DEREK NIMMO

My children were up early this morning – I had taken my normal Christmas Eve precaution of putting their clocks back two hours so that it would appear to be only four-thirty when it was in fact half past six. But my daughter, who seems to miss increasingly less these days, caught me at it and after I'd retired from her bedroom promptly reverted to British Standard Time.

Father Christmas, of course, behaved predictably. Last night the children, as always, had left beside their beds not only their stockings but also a glass of sherry and a mince-pie, something I always did as a child, too – to sort of refresh the old gentleman, help him on his toy-laden way. The happy thing is that, whilst he quite rightly drains the sherry glass, he always leaves half the mince-pie, which can then be pointed at as an example of moderation on a day of over-indulgence.

One tiny sadness, however, in the stocking opening. When the children's investigating fingers had reached the heel and by-passed the obligatory apple and orange they found for possibly the last time a shiny sixpence and a gleaming penny. In future, I suppose, even Christmas stockings will be decimalised. No great matter really, but it's strange how at Christmas one resents change. One wants the same old faces to be sitting around the same old table forever.

The order of battle for Christmas Day is in my family terribly constant. After church and the final great burst of

'Hark the Herald Angels' we visit friends, passing other groups of families similarly bound. My lot tend to look tolerably down at heel in relation to other people's relations as we don't open our presents until after lunch; and therefore do not have the sartorial advantage of all the matching tie and handkerchief sets and new scarves and handbags that pass one in the street.

Incidentally, all the walking part of this morning I enjoy immensely. Walking seems to have got a trifle out of fashion in recent years, but I have taken it up seriously again since a holiday I had this summer on a small island in the Hebrides. You know the joy of wandering through clean air with the silence only broken by the cries of gulls and terns and the breakers on the rocks beneath. And then coming back after a heavy day's tramping through bracken and heather to a tiny cottage and a log fire, and a miscellaneous collection of lanterns and candles, and then later sitting at twilight with a plate of freshly-gathered clams and a super cheese-sauce and watching the sun set over Loch Melford. Well, it's as near as I got to heaven this year.

Oh yes, except of course for Paros. Paros is another island and if you point a quick boat due south for about seven hours from Athens you should hit it. Well, we did anyway. And I'm enormously grateful, for here I was introduced to the joys of another form of transportation – mules. Now I'd always thought that mules had gone out with the Flight into Egypt, but no – waiting for me, well for us all really, on the quayside as we sailed in were Dimitracus and a large quantity of terribly available mules and donkeys for hire. Dimitracus insisted that out first trip should be to the Valley of a Million Butterflies and a hundred Nuns. Well, this to me was absolutely irresistible; although at first it looked as though there might be rather a frost, because the Sisters at the Convent were either on leave or noticeably under-strength. At last we reached the Butterflies which turned out not to be butterflies at all, but instead great scarlet moths. One shook the trees and thousands and thousands of them took to the air looking like a great host of scarlet angels.

Yes, that was pretty near to heaven too. And near to Christmas I suppose. I shall think about butterflies when I read in Church this morning, 'And suddenly there was with the Angel a multitude of heavenly host praising God and saying "Glory to God in the highest and on earth peace, goodwill to men".'

A very happy Christmas to you.

Sorting out Priorities

1. A Note on Paper
EUSTON MORE

About every 100,000 years or so, history takes a significant step forward. First, someone discovers fire. Then comes the wheel. Soon after that, paper. Has it ever occurred to you what bliss life would be without it? Well, my secretary knows, for one. It is not diesel fumes or tobacco or chronic bronchitis that is slowly killing her. It is paper. Every day she moves tons of it, mostly for no reason at all. She's absolutely withering away under the burden. We once worked out together during an office lull that she spent 84.5 per cent of her working day carrying paper about. The remainder of her time she spent typing – that is to say, creating paper for someone else to carry about.

Ever since paper was invented, we have been mesmerised by it. Consider the printer. I recently read in a business magazine that three-fifths of the nation's printers produce things like leaflets, selling goods we don't really need. Depth research had established that, on receipt of this material, addressees consigned it unread to the waste-paper basket. Conclusion: that three-fifths of the nation's printers could be profitably redeployed on jobs other than forging an unnecessary link between the paper mill and the dustbin. I don't know whether that's logic or not – anyway, it's research. But if that is the best we can manage out of one of the world's greatest discoveries, it makes us look pretty small, doesn't it?

This point was brought home to me recently when I went to see my solicitor about making my will. The first

thing he said was that he wanted 'to get it down on paper'.
I was much heartened at the time, for his method smacked of
brisk office efficiency and everything being tied up so that
there would be no doubt at all about where my wishes lay!

Months later, a single sheet of typing, double-spaced and
sealed with red wax, was presented to me for signature
before being consigned to a bank against the day my coffin
was on the drawing-board. Reading that document was indeed a salutary experience; it reduced taking out a mortgage
to the level of buying a bar of chocolate. As I posted it back,
I couldn't help thinking: is that how one ends up – a bit of
paper in a vault?

Because, in a way, that *is* how you are disposed of, isn't
it? When you are dead, you are broken up into bits of
furniture, perhaps a few pound notes, the odd piece of
jewellery and one or two miscellaneous and aged items
probably handed down to you from someone else. You
become a 'realisable asset', which is a pretty chilling sort
of thing to aim for.

But wait a minute: is that a true picture? At the end of life
have we no further contribution to make? Do we degener-
ate into something only fit to be squabbled over, or passed
on, perhaps as a wedding present, to someone our descend-
ants don't know very well, or maybe even 'popped' at a
neighbouring junk shop so that they can have an unexpected
holiday in Spain? Doesn't such a thought take one down a
peg or two? What about thinking it out again – with our
children in mind? They won't thank us for storing up things
like that for them, surely. They won't want to remember us
as a chair or a cupboard hanging on the wall. It's not very
constructive, is it, allowing ourselves to become a 'realisable
asset' by some obscure process of corporal metamorphosis?
The very thought of such a possibility must surely give us
pause.

Yes, it's quite a challenge, something we might well spend a little time doing our own research on now. For the things we can leave those who follow us that will be of use to them are things like the right kind of memories, good examples, abiding qualities and lasting values. Aren't *those* the legacies they'll need?

When I'd got as far as that with my thoughts, I reckoned it was time I went to see my solicitor again. This time about a codicil. After all, I felt sure he'd want 'to get it down on paper'.

2. Aspects of Beauty
MARTINE LEGGE

When I was young I was brought up to believe that striving to remain beautiful, youthful looking and fashionably dressed was the most important thing in a woman's life. That this brought you love, opportunities, status, respect, happiness. But I've lived in a world where I've seen several women grow old according to this philosophy and end their lives in bitterness, hatred and despair and, even more tragic, unable to understand why they were so miserable.

On the other hand I know how important it is to the morale to look one's best; how stupid to stop taking trouble over one's appearance, how pleasant to be admired and how delightful to look upon others who look good themselves. Just because a personal experience has caused me to feel sickened whenever I see an older woman who makes a fetish of her looks, this doesn't mean that I haven't seen many who are really beautiful, but their beauty has absolutely nothing to do with slavishly imitating the beauty of youth. Beauty, like achievement or love or truth, is a chameleon word that changes its colour according to who-

ever is using it; according to their age and state of understanding.

All my life I've listened to people arguing and making
facile value judgements and I've done the same myself,
believing implicitly in what I was saying each time. But
looking back, I now realise just how often I swung like a
weathercock from opinion A to opinion B and very often,
when there was no strong prevailing wind, I'd skelter
helplessly from opinion E to G to F like some novice skater
deprived of her supporting chair across the ice. This I
found infinitely distressing because I badly wanted to
believe in something fixed and safe which would really
show me the right way to go, once and for all.

Now that I'm older I've just started to learn a thing or
two and one of them is that you can't ever feel safe for long
because the whole business of living is about movement,
about development, and that most of this is done struggling
in the dark; that nothing fits into neat formulas, neither
love, beauty, ethics or morality, not even religion.

That great French novelist Marcel Proust said that most
people construct their house of life and then find they don't
fit in; it seems to have been built for someone quite different.
This makes sense because people are changing all the time,
spiritually as well as physically. That is what life is about, a
journey from A to B. But in order to develop positively
rather than merely changing, you have to be prepared to
recognise the changes as they occur and make your plans
accordingly.

It is hardly surprising that most people don't like doing
this because it often means the end of something they once
enjoyed and want to hang on to. Oddly enough, painful
though it is to give up the idea of being young, beautiful,
desirable, successful, having a good time, it is even harder to
face that great crisis of middle age which the psychologist

Jung described as the change from the ego-centred attitude of youth to the ego-transcending one of the second phase of life, from the subjective to the objective so to speak. The word 'crisis', however, is not as terrifying as it sounds. It comes from the Greek κρίνειν which means to decide, and it is this decision to accept a change in one's values which is often so very difficult.

To me this change and every change in one's life is what religion is all about. In the generic sense everyone has a religion because, fundamentally, religion is a person's concern for the meaning and purpose of his existence. I sometimes wonder whether it is not during the second half of life that we are meant to do our really important learning.

We are all brought up in today's society to look unremittingly for happiness in the form of pleasures considered valuable in themselves. Perhaps this is one of the reasons why the generations don't get on these days. By slavishly hanging on to the values of youth we forfeit respect of the young who are looking to us (often without knowing it) to provide them with some kind of map for the journey of life. Without us to guide them, to a certain extent, their future is even more precarious and uncertain than it might be otherwise.

It is wisdom and peace of mind and acceptance and understanding and the gentle withdrawal from the ego, from the material into the spiritual life, and the ensuing happiness that comes from fulfilling their destiny instead of fighting it off, that makes some old people so beautiful and such valuable friends.

3. Many Different Purposes
LEONARD NEAL

I've been asked to say what it is in Christianity that informs my working life. Now that's an extremely difficult question for people of my generation, for we have, in a curious way, taken some of the Christian precepts to heart rather more than others. For example, do you remember the story about the Pharisee who went to the Temple to pray aloud and to draw public attention to his devotion? This was used as an object lesson for us, in emphasising that Christianity is a personal religion, a personal and private compact with ourselves. And this has created an emphatic diffidence about the public testimony to a private faith, which makes many Britons of my age feel embarrassed and slightly resentful of being asked questions of this sort.

Perhaps another reason is that we grew up with the 'Gentle Jesus Meek and Mild' description of Christianity – of the stained-glass saints in the windows and the case-hardened saints in the pews. And with adolescence and manhood this concept seemed so much at variance with the realities of life as we were then finding them.

In the twenties and thirties there wasn't anything meek and mild about the aftermath of the First Great War with its poverty, its unemployment and its harshness. Yet few of us have utterly abandoned our religion, and all of us would admit, I think, that if life was lived according to Christian principles, then that life would be infinitely better and fuller than it is. For Christianity rejects all that's discreditable in our lives – that which we ourselves condemn: the conflict and the crime, the pollution, the selfishness and the sordidness.

So we are Christians really, and if so how should it inform our daily lives and influence our actions? Well, I'm a manager in one of the country's largest industries, and managers, I suppose, have a particularly difficult job of keeping so many different purposes in mind. On one side the needs of the enterprise to grow and be efficient and on the other the needs of ordinary people for rewards, for satisfaction and fulfilment in their work.

And so one goes to the office with the twin disadvantages of inherited diffidence in the face of inherent conflict. So how should Christianity inform one's daily life? Well, I've only time in this talk for one of its many precepts about treating others as we would like to be treated. And speaking for myself I'd like to be treated with courtesy and with respect. I'd like to be treated as an intelligent adult. I want to be trusted, I want to be given responsibility for my work and I want my boss, whoever he is, to set challenging standards in my work; standards, of course, that I can reach but which nevertheless extend me, so that, at the end of the day, I can look back on a testing experience out of which I came rather well. And if that happens I want my boss to notice it and to acknowledge it. I want this boss of mine to be someone I can respect who will be capable of stimulating loyalty in me, not only towards him but also towards the outfit that employs us both. It will be nice too, if he'll consider my feelings when things go wrong and not, just because I'm a subordinate, trample on me to relieve his own feelings. I'd also like him to keep me in the picture about policies and events that affect my job and also to listen to any views that I might have about them. Now, if I want these things for myself, why should not those who work for me want them as well; whether I'm just a manager or a shop steward or a trade-union official. Isn't that how Christianity informs our working lives?

4. The Uncut Cake

PATRICK PARRY OKEDEN

Some years ago I went to a christening party, and on the table was a beautiful iced christening cake and someone said, 'It seems a shame to cut it' and do you know they never did. We looked at it, admired it, and went home leaving it pure and unsullied, uncut. It still looked fine – but no one had any.

Cakes, or hot crusty loaves, or boxes of chocolates, bottles of beer, a Yorkshire pudding – it spoils them to use them – but they are no good if you don't and cakes are to be cut, and bottles are to be opened and bread to be broken – and people too – they are for sharing around.

But some people keep themselves to themselves. I went to see someone who wasn't in. I thought she might be ill so I knocked next door to ask and do you know the reply? 'I'm sorry I can't say – we haven't spoken for twenty years.' Well, that's keeping yourself to yourself all right. There's no risk of getting involved if you play it that way. And we do meet people who are like an uncut cake; neat, tidy, self-possessed and they give us nothing, we go away empty, they don't nourish.

Yet we have to recognise that it's difficult for some people to share themselves out – it's sometimes difficult for all of us. We have a fear of losing control of ourselves, of getting involved and being unable to pull out. It's rather like the physical fear of losing control of one's body or environment. I'm scared of diving into water – I fear the moment when I lose my balance and no longer have control, and a relationship does mean losing control of myself. It means I'm going to change. It means the other person will have power over me. I'm going to be involved and I don't know how it will end.

I was thinking how much I owe to people who do share themselves. All sorts of faces come into my mind – friends, people I've been to for help, colleagues, a teacher, my family – and I like to think I shared some of myself with them.

When I go to a wedding I never get over the astonishing thing that happens, the way the man and woman take themselves and their happiness and the next fifty years of their lives and put it all in each other's hands, at each other's mercy. For better, for worse, till death us do part. It seems to me the most amazing moment in a person's life, this risking your future on a relationship. No wonder some people fear to commit themselves and no wonder it takes some doing to work it out in practice so that some draw back into independent isolation and become married strangers. No wonder people often need help and that sometimes a marriage fails.

Marriage is an example of how risky it is to love. You have to abandon some of your self-possession, the private life you once had, the life that seemed no one else's business. It's like when a couple decide to have children. You abandon the tidy, free adult partnership which you can to some extent control and let yourself in for being taken over for years by children and all that they imply; broken nights, nappies, school, untidiness, anxiety, and enormous love and pride and joy. But your life isn't your own. You've risked it on a relationship and some don't, can't, daren't risk it. They keep themselves back from their family and the family back from the community.

A mother often gives herself by feeding her family – the most basic way of showing love – but of course she can also feed them instead of loving them. We can give things instead of ourselves. Presents can be gifts of love or gifts instead of love. Don't we hear so often, 'I can't think why they are so ungrateful, we've done everything for them, they had everything they wanted.' Sometimes we give our children everything they want except what they really want, and if we give things, not ourselves, we can't hide it.

Love has its risks, getting involved can be painful, but you can't have life without it. Cakes are for cutting, bread is for breaking, wine for drinking and life is given us to share.

5. It's No Concern of Mine
STANLEY KIRK

'It's no concern of mine.' I was so surprised and disappointed when he said that to me. You see, I was trying to help a boy of fourteen. Let me tell you about him.

He was born in prison because at the time his mother was serving a sentence. When he was weaned he was taken away, and he never saw his natural mother again. He was placed in a home with people far too old to cope with a sensitive, intelligent child. He became rebellious and very difficult. Persistently he refused to go to school. He not only truanted, but associated with the wrong kind of people, and as you would expect, found himself in trouble with the police.

Because of this, I thought a change to a new area might enable him to settle down, so I went to see the Headmaster in a different catchment area to try to persuade him to take this boy into his school. I explained I wanted if possible to prevent the lad from developing into a real criminal – you know that can so easily happen. It was then that the master looked at me and said, 'It's no concern of mine.' Of course, legally he was right, he could not be compelled to take this boy, and anyway why should he take a problem boy? Fortunately they aren't all like that.

As I left that school, a picture came to my mind of a story told by the Master of us all, of a lonely traveller who was assaulted and robbed, and left on the roadside to die. Now the very person from whom he could expect help came by on his way to church, but do you know, he was so religious and so engrossed in sacred things, even he said, 'This wounded man is no concern of mine.' Soon after, another came along: he was already late for church and felt he could not get involved. Anyway, why should he, it was not his responsibility.

We are then told that a man from a different country came that way, so he had a good excuse for doing nothing. But he was different, he had compassion, or to put it another way, he cared. So he did all he possibly could for the man. More than that, he passed him on to someone else who could do even more. So the wounded man received help and healing, and ultimately full restoration.

You will be glad to know I found a school willing to take the boy, where he did extremely well. I'm certain that school is richer for not only restoring a sick boy to perfect health, but also adding to the community a useful citizen, and this alone brings its own reward. Caring for others brings enrichment, purpose and meaning to life.

You can never tell how far-reaching a single act of kindness is. For example, a policeman on night duty found a parcel. It contained a baby boy and he was alive. No one ever claimed him. His identity remained unknown, so to give him a name they called him Thomas after the policeman who found him, and seeing he was found between two famous London bridges, they called him Thomas Bridges. Thomas proved to be an excellent pupil. Through study and hard work he ultimately became a doctor, and then, instead of devoting his life to making money, he became a missionary and spent the whole of his long life overseas.

All this was brought about because a policeman found an unwanted baby, and he didn't say, 'This is no concern of mine.'

6. Taking Trouble

A COUNTRY DOCTOR

It is a wonderful thing to be able to take trouble *away* from people. Health Visitors, nurses, doctors do it all the time – frequently effortlessly and unaware. Parents watch an ailing child get worse until their resources of common sense, faith and judgement are exhausted. They send for medical aid and a large part of their burden is lifted; they may still be anxious, but someone else with knowledge and experience greater than theirs is now responsible. Today doctors seem rarely to have time to sit and listen. Sitting and listening is the essential technique of The Samaritans, Alcoholics Anonymous and other life-saving voluntary organisations. I have a friend and patient who was very active in this field; prepared to drop everything in response to a telephone call, day or night, from someone he scarcely knew, to dash off and sit with him for a night, a day, two days if necessary: until the crisis was over. Now he is almost unbearably frustrated by physical disabilities and he often needs oxygen to get from his bed to his easy chair. Yet people in trouble still come to see him and come away feeling better.

Some of us go to pieces if the budgerigar dies; some get violently abusive and blame everyone in sight to avoid taking the trouble on ourselves; some take trouble with such cheerfulness, dignity and lack of self-pity that they are an inspiration to others. Of the many in this latter group I have attended, two very different mothers spring to mind.

The first was a farmer's wife whose fifth child was born quite deaf. Will you try to imagine what it is like to teach a child, who can hear *nothing*, to talk and then to read? It takes years to train an expert to do that and they may spend years on a child to achieve it. That woman had a long, hard day, seven days a week. But every night for three years, after everyone else had gone to sleep, she took that baby out of his cot and without any training or tuition she taught him to speak – by touch, by facial expression, by letting him feel her breath and touch her lips and her throat; but most of all by almost unbelievable patience and loving care.

I first saw the second woman shortly after she arrived in our little town, having married a local boy; she was waiting for a bus and she stood out like a butterfly on a dull, grey day. Her blonde hair was piled high above her pretty face, she had a beautiful figure and her tiny, flared skirt was like a frill above her long, lovely legs.

A few months later she came to my surgery to announce that she was pregnant. My heart sank as I guessed how much time and trouble she would have to take each day to maintain that elaborately made-up face, those long painted nails. How would she look after a few weeks of caring for a baby? Was she the sort of girl who could possibly do the sordid chores the job entailed? I also assumed, God forgive me, that the pregnancy was unwanted. I was wrong on all counts.

The labour was prolonged and complicated, and she stuck it well but came back from hospital with her baby girl's legs kept in a frog-like position by clumsy plaster splints. Bathing and changing a new baby can be a nightmare to the novice even when everything is normal. She did it all beautifully. And her lovely smile was even more frequent, because of smiling at the baby.

Then the baby began to have fits. Feeding was difficult and in addition she had somehow to get about twelve doses of medicine down a day. Eventually she had to be told the worst news probably that a woman is ever called on to hear –

her little girl was one of those mercifully rare distortions of creation – she had been born without a mind; she would never be able to understand or manipulate the world in which she found herself; she would never be able to talk, or walk, or think.

I have seen that mother in her own home and know how very near she has been to complete heartbreak. But she pushes the pram down our High Street as lovely and as carefully turned-out as ever. Everyone smiles at her; and they smile at the baby. And they both smile right back at everyone. And when I drive through the town and meet her, flaming up the street, and she smiles and waves, I feel a sudden burst of joy mixed with shame at how ungrateful I can be in my own trouble-free life.

How she does it I do not know. But this I know: there is a limit to the amount you can comprehend with the intelligence you have been given; there is a limit to how much you can achieve with the strength in your muscles. But there is no limit to how much trouble you can take if you really care. No limit at all.

7. Love and Discipline
JOHN RAE

There is a definition of maturity that I like very much. It is that the mature person is able to give out love in greater measure than he needs to receive it. What I like about this definition is that it suggests a relationship between love and discipline, an unusual association of words and one that is probably not popular today. Yet love that is undisciplined is immature and almost certainly self-indulgent.

It is the fashion no doubt to believe that love is only possible by dropping as many controls and as many clothes as possible. Love is very much more than being uninhibited, and very much more than just self-indulgence. Mature love can never be self-indulgent, but must always be based on self-discipline. To sacrifice oneself for someone else, or for a wider cause of humanity, cannot be done by self-indulgence. The whole drift of our times encourages the opposite view, that love can be achieved just by falling into it, that all you need is love. And when this trite and facile view proves to be wrong then there is frustration and bitterness. In fact, that is just the frustration of finding that love without discipline does not work, does not bring happiness in human relations. And needless to say does not bring in the day of the brotherhood of all mankind.

The reaction to this frustration may be revolutionary cant, or cynical materialism, so that 'love is all you need' is a heresy. Perhaps the moral equivalent of the 'get rich quick' philosophy, which is a heresy in its own right.

And just as love is a discipline, so discipline is, or should be, an expression of love. It is easy to see that parents who fail to instil some understanding of the need for self-discipline in their children are being irresponsible. But I wonder whether they are not being rather more than just irresponsible.

When we look back at our Victorian forebears, we are inclined to think that they brought up their children in a very cruel fashion, that they had little to do with them, that they denied their children the ordinary pleasures of life, and that they treated them often with physical cruelty. But I wonder whether people in another century who look back upon our times will not come to a similar conclusion for different reasons – that we are being cruel to our children. That in a more subtle way perhaps than the Victorians, we are harming their personalities perhaps for life, because we are allowing them to be self-indulgent. In the home, as in other areas of life, it may well be that 'no' is more often an expression of love than 'yes'. In other words, that the parent who really loves his or her child will be prepared to say no on more occasions than is common nowadays.

And then if we link this to the thought of God's love perhaps the same thing applies – that God in his desire to encourage in us the self-discipline that will make us mature adults says to us 'no', tries to prevent us from the sort of self-indulgence that will produce unhappiness and frustration, and that will prevent us being able to develop that self-discipline without which we are incapable of loving our fellow human beings.

So love is discipline, and discipline should be an expression of love. I think that the two words do belong together after all.

8. Argument

VIVIAN OGILVIE

I once found myself sitting next to two men who had fallen into conversation about the way to establish peace. Each of them had a different recipe. One believed that peace would come if only the sale of armaments were stopped. The other thought it would come if only the women of the world would unite to demand it.

I state that they had fallen into conversation. It would be more accurate to say that they were engaged in alternating monologues. One would go on for a bit about armaments, then the other would break in, 'You're quite right. If only all the women in the world would unite, we should have peace,' and he would go on about that for a while. Then, after a decent interval, the other would interrupt him, 'You're absolutely right. If the sale of armaments were stopped we could have peace tomorrow.'

They were a couple of amiable crackpots. But I think we are all inclined to acquire a hobby-horse and then lose sight of everything else. We find some cause which we come to see as supremely important. Or our eyes are opened to some great wrong, some great evil. And we easily slide into a state of mind in which we no longer acknowledge the existence of any other rights or wrongs. There's only our one.

We can all see this clearly enough in cases which don't capture our sympathies. Many of us would say that the champions of various forms of puritanical restriction are prone to this fault. But when it comes to causes we ourselves agree with, our principles may begin to wobble. We may, for instance, feel very strongly about the oppression of coloured people. And before we know where we are, we may have decided that, because we disapprove of Apartheid, other people must not be allowed to play games against South Africans. And we have slipped into precisely the position for which we would criticise the Lord's Day Observance people.

Demonstrations obviously tend to cultivate a one-eyed view of rights and wrongs. We may loathe what the Americans have been doing in Vietnam. I do; but does this mean that some unknown shopkeeper or motorist has ceased to have any rights and I'm entitled to heave a brick through the shopkeeper's window and set fire to the motorist's car? Just to show what an unselfish idealist I am? There are other principles and causes besides whatever's happened to catch my attention. Whoever we are, we are eminently liable to kid ourselves about our motives, and fancy that we are being high-minded when we are really indulging a taste for self-assertion.

And what if the good cause which we invoke to sanction our activity is not the rights or wrongs of some other people, but what we believe to be our own: if the issue is *my* grievance, *my* rights? This is surely where our talent for self-deception is only too likely to run away with us. My mates and I feel that we are underpaid, let's say. So we'll go on strike. And we proclaim a sacred principle – the right of every man to withdraw his labour. There's no denying this principle. Everyone has the right to withdraw his labour if he's dissatisfied: everyone, including hospital nurses and doctors, even the surgeon in the operating theatre who's suddenly fed up with the National Health Service. 'Oh, wait a minute,' you may say. 'The patient has some rights too, you know.' That's just my point. My right to withdraw my labour is not the only right. There are always other people to be considered. In some recent situations, for example: people who had nowhere to put their rubbish, people whose only heating was electric, handicapped people who couldn't use the staircase and had relied on the lift; children who ought to have been con- tinuing their education, out-patients who needed to go to hospital for treatment, mourners who wanted to bury their dead. It isn't self-evident that all these forfeited their rights, once some men felt entitled to a rise.

You get my point. There's never only one right, only one good cause, only one wrong to be remedied. Perhaps St Paul had this in mind when he wrote, 'Look not every man on his own things, but every man also on the things of others.'

9. Communication
CYRIL FLETCHER

On the day that I had the invitation from my producer to assemble some thoughts on getting through to other people, I read in the morning paper of some young people, seventeen and eighteen years old, it was thought, who had raided the compound where some pets were kept for mentally handicapped people. These pets had been most callously murdered and a small goat had been knifed almost to death.

I cannot understand the mentality of any vandalism. To destroy what it has taken time and trouble and loving care (in some instances) to build, I find beyond any comprehension. Wantonly to kill innocent little animals, and also animals which were giving some kind of pleasure and comfort to stricken fellow mortals (for whom those youths should be feeling compassion), made me quite ill with horror and weak with that numb feeling of despair that I always feel about war, and man-made senseless hurt to man.

How has this lack of feeling come about? Obviously to start with the parent cannot have got through any kind of feelings to the child. Either the parent was brutish, or subnormal, or was never there when that child needed love and understanding. When at school, this child could never have been taught right from wrong and the difference between love and hate, or love and not-love. And I'm going to throw in here that it is all very well to suggest that all religion should be kept out of schools but is it not possible that the simple story of christianity and christian love expounded with sympathy might have got through to these vandals? Not every one of these youths could possibly be of the same awful pattern of inhumanity. There must have been one amongst them who knew he was doing wrong, and who suppressed his own feelings whilst running with the herd.

Prison warders and doctors and chaplains and governors have this same trouble of communication. They are so frequently faced with a blank wall of animal, unthinking, brute mulishness. And it is their job to try and find a way to communicate, their job to seize on some small tangible glimmer of the humanity which is in all of us . . . it is their job (and what a thankless and painstaking job it has to be sometimes) to find the spark and to fan it to a flame.

There is the awful responsibility of the spoken word. And so often in trying to get through to other people, and sometimes in absolute sincere desire for doing good, the wrong words are said and the wrong impression is made. When you are trying to communicate you have to try so hard to get into the skin of the other man. You have to realise the size of his understanding. To realise the narrowness sometimes of his vision. The size of his kind of life and existence compared with yours. This is an almost impossible thing to do, yet if you are to have any kind of exchange of thought and feeling this is absolutely essential. Before you begin to talk. Before you start to communicate you will have to marshal all your facts, all your feelings, understand the whole of your background and the whole of his background . . . and all these facts and surmises and suppositions you will have to have by heart . . . and I mean by *heart* . . . like a barrister's brief. Even then only time will tell whether you have got through, and whether you have got through the right way.

In this highly mechanical world, in these times when man has this almost unbelievable, almost magical technical skill he does not seem to be able to get through any better than he ever did. With radio and television, the telephone and the printing press we do not seem able to send out sense and sensibility with the direct sureness that eleven illiterate men did who first spread to a hungry world on foot, and by word of mouth, the message of Christ's love.

10. Receiving

FRED BROWN

I've come to the conclusion that far too many of us are trying too hard to accumulate things. It's dead easy. You work a bit harder, save your money and make your purchase. Colour tv, car, house! Fair enough, if you want, really want, hard enough you'll get them. For most of us it's only a question of time. But what then? Funny thing – have you noticed? – this business of accumulating things. The more you get the more you want. Mark you, I'm not against getting things. I wouldn't say no to a few more myself.

The fact remains, though, that it's possible to get more and more, and to receive less and less, by which I mean that some of us are in danger (put it no stronger than that), of getting plenty of almost everything money can buy while possessing hardly anything that money can't. It's really the difference between the world outside ourselves and inside.

In the world outside the goods pile up with the years and tell their own story of success. But the world inside ourselves is another matter. There, money doesn't talk. We either have the capacity to receive or we stay impoverished. Most of us do, stay impoverished, I mean. And it's not because we're wicked or antisocial or even more deliberately selfish than the next man. It's just that we've lost our way and don't know it. We don't see what's happening to us. In fact, we see hardly anything.

Some of us look at a flower, a sunset, the sky at night, and see nothing. The telly's more real anyway. We provide handsomely for our families but seem unable to enjoy them, to know them as real people. It's rather like a man having the money to buy, or even the skill to make, a musical instrument but not the spirit to be thrilled by the lovely music it helps to play; or a woman caught up in a round of endless gaiety but knowing that she's only a social butterfly, flitting from one empty experience to another.

I wish I could be more precise about what I mean. But this capacity to receive as distinct from accumulate things is hard in some ways to understand, let alone describe. The most surprising people have it. Some are rich, others poor. Some healthy, others chronically sick or handicapped. Some escape trouble, others get more than their share. The one thing they have in common is what I can only call their outlook or attitude to life. And that, I realise, sounds a bit corny. Even pompous or platitudinous.

The interesting thing is that when you talk to people who know how to receive in the way I suggested, you quickly get the point that they didn't consciously learn how to receive at all. As long as we gear our life to winning favours and buying, getting, accumulating – we're all the time destroying our capacity to receive the things that money can't buy. It happens naturally.

But there are individuals, not necessarily religious in any orthodox sense, who, I've noticed, put people first; not things but people, always people first. This probably explains why their love, like their appreciation of beauty and goodness, grows with the years and enables them to receive more and more. I can't think of any other explanation. I don't know how else to put it. What I do know is that such people really live (continue to receive) till they die.

11. Accepting
ROGER GAUNT

George is not any easier to live with since he got his Rover. The rich and those who have what they apparently want are also troubled, not through lack of valuable things to possess outside, but through fear of there being nothing inside of value. The trouble with Jane is not that she has no washing-machine, but she has no confidence in herself. Martin – it's not that he has been passed over for a company car, but that he dare not confront the Area Manager and tell him what he thinks. The problem is not external riches, but an internal feeling of 'I'm no good inside'.

It does seem to me that Jesus sees the problem like that. He says, 'Don't fill the gap with things, but face the gap, look at what's there. You aren't seeing properly what's there. How many loaves have you?' His friends said, 'We can't possibly feed this crowd, we've got no resources.' 'Go and look again,' he says. 'Well, just a few loaves and two fish. How's that?' 'That'll do very well for a start.' And it does still.

I think this is what the Gospel is, that God is able to make a satisfactory job of what's already there, already within you. Just as in an examination it's not always lack of information that counts against me, but it's because I just can't see the relevance of a lot I already know. I just can't get hold of it. I must see the relevance of and accept what's in me already. That, I suppose, includes my hostility to people, my great need to be on top, to be admired.

George is hard to live with, not because he has brake trouble, but because he's surrounded by unaccepting people who'd like him to be different. And Jane is so depressed because she's pressured to live up to her husband's expectation, which she can't manage.

It is my belief that God accepts us as we actually are now. God believes in me, and my unending capacity to grow. God warms into life that which I already am, and He forgives without condition George and Jane and you.

Mary believed this and became the mother of Jesus.

Ash Wednesday

PETER FIRTH

Most of us are very inadequate so far as most things are concerned. How many of you listening can drive a train, lecture in Greek, feed a computer, weave cloth, remove an appendix, or play the harp? How many of you can actually bring up, or have actually brought up, a family in the best possible way? And aware of all the shortcomings and failures, it still can remain accurate and yet a relief to say, 'Oh I'm hopeless at bringing up children'.

Today is Ash Wednesday. Ashes to ashes, dust to dust, says the Church. Dust thou art, and to dust shalt thou return, a minister has said over millions of people today, and then he's marked them on the forehead with the ashes of last year's Palm crosses, burned yesterday.

And thousands of lines of people have knelt in this great general confession of failure and frailty – have remembered that they will die one day, that they have made a mess of many things. And they have confessed this in public. If they had stood out in the road, and told the neighbours that they had made a mess of things, they would have been looked at as weird, they would have felt ridiculous. But in a ritual action, which stretches across the five continents, they have made a public matter of that which all of us know privately – that we're very frail creatures really, failures in what we really believe, falling short even of the standards that we set ourselves.

Now to my mind, it's one of the church's reasons for

existence, to provide a kind of framework within which people can admit that they are fallible – not least in the business of living. And when a Christian minister looks down his church at the time of the general confession and hears all those people telling God that they are fallible, it is one of the most moving experiences in life. People need to say it, because in the job of living most of us leave much to be desired. And it helps to have some sort of ritual way of saying it, both to ourselves, and to each other, and to God.

Today, as I said, is Ash Wednesday. On most days of the year if you told somebody they had got some dirt on their face, they would feel slightly insulted, they would certainly feel they had lost face. But today it might be a smudge of ash. And although it represents an admission of failure, or guilt, I do not think they would mind if you knew it. Because the ritual has enabled them to say, 'I know I am inadequate – that is why I need your understanding – your love.'

Family Living

1. The Need to be Nasty
PATRICK PARRY OKEDEN

Do you know that time, towards the end of Christmas Day, when the goodwill sometimes runs out? Exhausted parents flop in their chairs among the debris; children, bloated but cheerful, play with their new possessions on the rug; and then, all of a sudden, all hell breaks loose. Children start to fight, there are tears and tantrums, someone's new toy gets broken and it will be surprising if parents don't lose their tempers too – with each other and the children.

The goodwill has run out. It has been a strain being kind and grateful and feeling that everything must be enjoyed. We can't keep up being nice any more; it's time to be nasty, to be ungrateful, unkind. Adult or child we probably feel we hate our rotten family, and if not on Christmas Day, then certainly we feel it sometimes.

I think this is one of the best things about families – that you can hate them, one at a time or the whole damn lot at once. You can be nasty, really nasty, and they will still be around tomorrow when you love them.

For instance: you can come home from school after a difficult day and refuse your tea, or fly off the handle and slam doors. You can come home from work full of depression or suppressed fury and find fault with your wife and children and be a bear with a sore head. You can have a rotten day at home stuck with chores and be thoroughly nasty to the family: and they may fight back, or tell you what they think or just take it – but with any luck they will take it and be around to be nice to later.

E

I know plenty of people who will accept me when I'm being nice, when I'm trying hard, when I'm on my best behaviour. But I have a sneaking feeling that if they knew the worse side of my nature the smile of welcome would pretty soon freeze. I don't feel at all sure if I am really acceptable – because I also need to be nasty, to be bad-tempered, to be difficult, to express the frustration and the unhappiness and the anger which are part of every person's experience.

And that's where a family comes in. A family will not only allow me to show my better self – it will allow me to be my worse self. At home my feelings are almost sure to emerge – at home I can sometimes be bad-tempered, un-grateful, sulky, miserable – I can be nasty – and still be put up with. And that seems to me one of the best things a person or a group of people can do for another – allow someone to be at their worst and still care about them and not walk out.

Parents can do this for children and children can also do it for their parents. A widow speaking on the radio the other day told how her grief at the loss of her husband would take the form sometimes of bad temper – of picking on her children – and how the children would accept it, and help her through it.

Husbands and wives can do this for each other. A woman once told me how her husband in a painful illness used to swear at her and say the most hurtful things: he didn't do this in front of the doctor – only to her, because she loved him, and to her he was able to express the terrible hurt and bitterness inside him: and she was able to take it and bear the pain of it with him. It seemed a wonderful thing for one person to do for another.

A family can be like a trampoline. It can absorb the shocks of our worst moments, our ghastly failures, our antisocial behaviour and keep sending us back to meet life. We need it when we're small and have to find someone to take our frustration and rage – we need it in adolescence when we're mixed up and moody and rebellious and so often need to be difficult. We need it all through life, and people on their own desperately need others who will accept them in this kind of way. It's a terrible loss when someone grows up without a family: but it is also a loss when a family cannot take the strain of our need to be nasty: when we aren't allowed to feel hate for our parents or jealous of our brother or sister, or when a family closes its ranks to exclude the one who behaves too badly.

I think my family is marvellous, and not least because when I am moody and difficult, when I find fault with every-one, then they tell me how impossible I am, but they still stick around, they make me feel I matter in spite of it, and they should know, because they've seen me at my worst. In fact they love me enough to allow me to be nasty – and who will do that for me, except the infuriating family that I love so much?

2. Maternity

BERNADINE BISHOP

Consider this advertisement: 'Wanted. Young person to act as nursery nurse, playleader, psychologist, cook, weight-lifter, medical expert, nightwatcher, accident prevention officer and general organiser. Permanent position of the utmost responsibility. No supervision. 168-hour week. No experience or qualifications required.'

Of course we never see such an advertisement, and if we did we should be puzzled and worried. But on the other

hand we are not puzzled and worried when a young girl
lightly answers the responsibilities of motherhood. There
is no other task so vast and so open-ended which anyone
takes on with so little preparation as maternity.

When I was expecting my first child – and I'm sure I was
typical in this way – I was intensely preoccupied with the
excitement and the wonder of it, but my feelings were much
more concerned with myself than with my baby. I was
wrapped up in the experience of pregnancy as such. Of
course I planned for the baby, and of course I read books on
child care; but I don't remember giving much thought to
the long-term future. My imagination did not really go
beyond the new-born stage, although at times I may have
dimly discerned a toddler, incredibly far ahead. We talk
about expecting a baby, never about expecting a person, and
my emotional experience certainly didn't get beyond expecting a baby. The schoolchild, the examinee, the employee,
the parent, the independent being – it never really dawned
on me that that was what I was expecting.

People say jokingly that no one would ever have children
if they realised beforehand what they were letting themselves
in for. Of course this is untrue. But I think it's true that you
can only learn after the event what you have let yourself in
for. Even then you only discover by degrees. You only
find out gradually that parental love is a life-sentence. I
don't think the dewy-eyed young couple choosing a pram
realise that they are going to have its occupant somewhere
in their minds until the day they die.

Since child psychology started, it has always been taken
for granted that the best thing for the young child is to be
with his mother as much as possible. Now for the first
time the value of that relationship seems to be coming under
fire. On the one hand some sociologists are throwing doubt
on the need of a child for a close-knit family circle, and seem

to think something more communal might be better. And on the other hand, Women's Liberationists are demanding round-the-clock nursery facilities for young children, which if they get it will obviously lead to a slackening of the mother–child bond. My first reaction is – how terrible! But I wonder if it would really be so bad. I've been trying to think out what differences the toning down of that relationship would make to a child.

While thinking about it I was watching one of my own boys out of the window trying to teach himself to roller-skate. He was falling over again and again and picking himself up and trying again with great persistence. Other people he knows well went past from time to time and gave a word of congratulation or sympathy. Somehow I knew that if I appeared the next fall would lead to tears and fury and discouragement. The mood of independent perseverance would somehow be broken. Now I don't think (I hope not, anyway) that this is something special to my own relationship with my son. I seem to have observed the same sort of thing with other mothers and their children. Supposing a child was looked after in a group, comprising plenty of other grown-ups besides his own parents, so that he had a lot of friendly well-wishers but no intense relationship, perhaps he would have fewer bouts of anger and self-pity. That looks at first glance like a good thing; but what would happen to all his violent moods and anxious tendencies, which often seem to be brought out in his relationship with mum? After all, we all have them. They would hardly disappear just because there was no context in which he felt he could let them rip.

I suspect the intensity of the mother–child relationship brings things out in the child – both good and bad things – that otherwise wouldn't emerge, extending his personality both ways. I'm sure it extends the personality of the mother.

3. Children Leaving Home
JEAN RICHARDSON

Yesterday, after having spent a weekend at home, my son thanked me for having him. It was one of the saddest moments of my life because it summed up the subtly different relationship between us now that he's left home.

When he went up to University, the excitement of getting everything ready, packing his trunk, driving up on a lovely autumn afternoon and installing him in his college rooms, kept me going right up to the time I arrived back. But then I went into his empty bedroom, so unnaturally tidy and bare, and the full force of it hit me. He'd gone. It was then that I began to imagine.

Suppose he started taking drugs? Suppose that he got so lonely he turned on the gas fire without lighting it? Suppose some horrible girl got him into trouble? Suppose he fell in the river? If I'd stopped to think rationally, I'd have realised that it was highly unlikely that he'd do all these things, particularly as he is of a somewhat cautious disposition, but just then I had a very vivid picture of him dying from all four possibilities.

When my second son followed him, three years later, I didn't have quite the same feelings of alarm – by that time I'd come to know the student set-up better and to fear it less – but back home again, in *his* empty room, I felt the same pangs of apprehension. However would he cope, this absent-minded, un-with-it boy of mine, to remember to do his washing, manage his money or get himself to lectures on time? – forgetting that he'd quite successfully hitched his way through Greece and Turkey with nothing more than a change of underwear and a packet of liquorice allsorts.

One thing I did know and never pretended to myself to be otherwise – both boys had gone. And I mean gone. Oh yes, they'd come back, stay a few days, a few weeks per-haps, but they had left home mentally. There is a sadness in this – the breakup of a family unit – and no one feels it more than my youngest son who misses his brothers very much. But I'm comforted by the sense of the rightness of it. This is as it should be, they've been looked after and brought up thus far upon their way and now they are ready and able to go forward into life on their own.

And I think it is important to understand that they no longer want me to be responsible for them – to worry over them, plan for them, even think about them too much. It's accepted that we all write or ring each other when we feel like it or need anything, and I find we're all in touch fairly regularly, if only to say everything's all right – after all, that's all we really *need* to know.

Sometimes I find myself missing them more than usual, but on the other hand it's lovely to be able to relax; not only physically, though that's welcome, but it's such a relief not to have to keep up with them, or be a good ex-ample, or try to influence them any more. And it's refreshing to have time to get to know myself again. So much of bringing up children is having to pretend. Of course, this is necessary and not a bad thing, but after years of echoing Dr Spock, Freud and the Bible, I found I'd almost lost sight of myself. It isn't easy to face the fact that your children have outgrown you. For most of us it involves a time of painful readjustment in our suddenly empty homes particu-larly if, like me, you have no husband, but I've found that to be able to let them go, cheerfully, trustfully – and un-reservedly, results in a closer understanding, a much more carefree relationship and a true freedom all round. And it's lovely when they *do* come home!

4. The Only Child
TOM HETHERINGTON

I am the only child of my parents and the parent of an only child. But my father was one of seven, my mother one of eight, and my wife has four brothers, so I have at least had opportunities for close observation of the most fascinating of all social units – *the family*. I don't know what it feels like to be one of several brothers and sisters, or even the parent of such a brood.

To me a family is a curious spectacle. The frankness of the members to each other is appalling to an only child. They have been used to each other's existence since early consciousness, and think nothing of it, but the only child has no one with whom to share this very healthy privilege of instantaneous outspoken comment. The members don't treat it as a privilege, as one of the family 'perks' – they seem to think each other a bit of a nuisance most of the time.

The problem the only child has to face in the family committee when he is small is that he usually feels himself outvoted 2 to 1. As he grows through his teens there may be shifting changes in alignment between the three members. Nothing serious, but possibly an undercurrent of discomfort not noticeable in the stormier seas of life in a large family. And yet, in its own way, there can be no more warming, more delightful, more intimate family relationship than two parents and a daughter or son, in affectionate harmony with each other.

I was interviewing a boy for college recently, and he *was* a boy. At seventeen he should have been a young man. To me he demonstrated the dangers of the one-child family. He was an only son, very happy in his home, obviously very comfortable, his only pastime fishing on his own, and no personal friends. He was very anxious to get into the college nearest to his home, so that he could be a day student and travel home every night. He looked quite uncomprehending when I asked if he had thought of being more venturesome and going further afield. He was used to going home from school. This was what he wanted to do at college – and, I suspect, it was what he would continue to do when he became a teacher.

I couldn't help worrying about his future for he was a boy never fully weaned. And such cases are not uncommon. I should add, of course, that there are plenty of well-matured youngsters who can safely attend the local college without loss to themselves.

An only child has a chance to think, to be alone, to discover himself in a way which is rarely possible for a member of a larger family. Considering the pressures of adult life, this in retrospect can seem an enchanted period. It seemed to me all the world stood still while I listened to it tick. An only child has the chance to explore, discover and reflect without the pushings and pullings of people around him.

The only child is sometimes the lonely child, but with luck he will learn a lesson of great price – the ability to stand on his own two feet without reliance on anyone – if he is not smothered by over-indulgent parents, if they have the wisdom not to ruin his sense of values by showering on him enough money and presents to share among a large family. If they do make this mistake, he's going to have a tough start to married life.

5. Hearing Their Prayers
BA MASON

As my children grow up and away there are some aspects of the mother–child relationship which begin to seem, to me, so wildly improbable as to be downright impossible.

Did this son, with his side-whiskers and his wife and his huge great feet, ever really embroider a little crooked square of canvas with HOME SWEET HOME and bring it back to me from school? Was it possible that I ever sharply corrected this elder one, now so sophisticated and censorious, for his sloppy table manners? How could I have summoned enough strength of character and authority to have forced this third giant, against his will, into attending classes for Scottish country dancing, and thus ruin the whole of one of his Easter holidays? It just doesn't seem believable now, any more than, looking at the three of them today, I can believe that I used to hear their prayers.

But I did. Every single evening, week in, week out, after their bath and the story and their various trumped-up subterfuges about aches and pains and thirst and inexplicable fears had been dismissed, they all three said their prayers; and I heard them. It was like a knot tied neatly round the end of their day, sending them off to sleep, parcelled secure-ly, stamped with spiritual grace.

I'm not the most maternal of women, and I shan't dream of enlarging on how angelic my children could look then, clean in striped pyjamas, reeking of toothpaste, their hair neatly brushed the way I liked it brushed (and still think it looks nicest), their hands folded, eyes shut and voices piping away. Anyway, I wasn't looking at them. I was slumped on my knees by one bed after another, so tired by then that this brief moment was like a full stop of dark and peace, my spinning head firmly buried in my hands, my eyes shut and my brain alert only for mechanical correction if any of them forgot a bit.

I've said before, and I haven't changed, that having my children grown up is a great joy to me. When they were little and utterly dependent, my responsibility to and for them was a great pressure on me. I was frightened by this responsibility, and perhaps I took it all too seriously, but these were the first human creatures who had ever been in my complete control and first their helplessness and later their careless disregard for danger kept me in a permanent state of tension and strain. I was frightened of misusing my responsibility and nervous of not recognising the truth where the children were concerned and so acting in error.

That little bit of prayer hearing helped me. It was a peaceful moment and often, up till then, the day had been far from peaceful; and I knew that the next day, and the next and the next weren't going to be peaceful either. I felt a feeling of safety, however temporary; all who've had children know how quickly the safe feeling can be blown into a million fragments by a sudden piercing cry; or violent sickness; or just a furious primitive fight blown up from nowhere like a summer storm. Hearing their prayers used to make me feel happy that I'd got them through another day, that nothing awful could happen to them for a little while, we were all safe at home, the roof four-square over us, and thank God for it, and now perhaps they'd go off and get the sleep they needed to keep them strong and well. I think a hen feels much the same, prodding the last egg into position with her scaly foot and settling down for a spell of peace and quiet at last on top of her clutch.

I think that now I can recognise that I was, unconsciously, resting my burden, beloved but still a burden, on someone better fitted to cope with it. No, that's not right because I was the one to cope with it, and I did, but I was resting it on someone who understood about it.

I've said I'm not very maternal, nor am I very religious, but I believe in my God, who is loving and sorry for me, even if He is powerless to stop evil; one who can't – not won't – stretch out His hand to protect me and the people

I love. Why should He? And I don't expect Him to. But I need Him to be sorry and to understand. Pity is a great stiffener of my sinews and understanding is what we all crave.

Looking back, I miss those moments, now I come to think about it. I didn't feel the children and I were divinely plugged in to anyone but I think, perhaps, I was feeling the peace of God, something only too rarely found by me.

Holy Week

RUTH PITTER

We do live in terrible times. But there is a big credit side to that account. One very big item on the credit side is our greatly increased scientific knowledge, honesty and accuracy. New and wonderful methods have been invented, vast quantities of new material discovered; learning has been subsidised, and countless minds illuminated. So that where it took tremendous courage even a hundred years ago – courage which very few possessed – to say, 'The truth at any price, so far as we can find it,' I really believe a majority of civilised people would gladly say it now. All the same, we must bear in mind that not every kind of truth can be investigated or discovered scientifically. Neither honest faith, nor for that matter, honest doubt nor honest unbelief is subject to that discipline.

It is hard to realise that only a century or two ago people held that the universe was only a few thousand years old. What a time-scale we have unrolled since then! At least, there seems to be a lot more of it. A lot more past, and perhaps a lot more future; perhaps. But past and future are queer things. The past is over and done; we can't alter it. The future is still to come; we can't anticipate it. Only the present moment is real. William Blake called it 'eternity's sunrise'. The present moment is our little bit of eternity. So in speaking of our faith, though I don't forget the picture in the past, the picture in history, I like to use the present tense as much as possible, because the things of faith are in the eternities, and the present is as near as we can get, what with only being able to think in three dimensions, and all that sort of thing.

There are things we all push away from ourselves with all our might. Pain-killers and sedatives for the least twinge of body or mind. All sorts of commercialised luxuries to counteract our sense of lack or inferiority. Drugs to make death easy. Refined and tactful funerals to spare us the grim details. Permissiveness for the things we want to do, and permissiveness to avoid the things we don't want to think of. But Christ refused the anaesthetic He was offered.

Now I do believe that it's one of the great glories of modern medicine and surgery that pain has been so largely conquered. But pain is a fact of nature. It may well be that there is a lot to be learned from it. Don't mistake me here. I'm not thinking of the perverted association of pain with voluptuousness. But of pain, mental and physical, as a legitimate part of what it means to be a person.

I am a poor creature indeed compared with the Christian martyrs, but I did have some very severe pain myself once. The doctor was quite apologetic. It was a thing they would so gladly spare the patient, he said, if they could; but so far they hadn't found any way to do so. But afterwards I wondered if it wasn't better to have the pain. There was such astonishment in it, for one thing. It was Experience with a capital E. I thought, 'Nobody knows anything who hasn't had a pain like that.' It quite altered my character for a bit; I felt miraculously enlightened, and I had so much more moral courage; I felt I could clear up the misunderstandings of a lifetime. The improvement wore off, I'm sorry to say, but it was a great landmark in my life, and at least the memory of it has lasted. To me, it was a tiny sample of the way in which the martyrs are placed beyond life's ordinary concerns and given some kind of supernatural strength. And grief too; it is so often our griefs which make us grow up. While as for death, coming to terms with that, our own death and the deaths of our friends – that is the business of a whole lifetime, beginning perhaps in a blind terror or a blind avoidance of the very idea, and ending, if all goes well, in a creative acceptance, a facing of our natural end. I wonder, is death something we have to do, like Him, rather than something we must just go through without knowing anything about it?

And now it is all over. His Body is entombed. The little group of pupils and close friends is scattered, in hiding, fearful for their own lives. Almost they have ceased to believe in Him. (As C. S. Lewis pointed out, they never quite saw what He meant by His kingdom, anyway.) The women who hung about the place of execution now hang about the place of burial, like bewildered birds about their robbed and ruined nest. They have lost Love's own Lord, the incarnate meaning of all that gives life *any* meaning.

In so many lives, even the most loving and pious, there is this dark night – Jesus himself encountered it on the Cross. But there is always work for women to do, even in deepest trouble. They collect their spices and their linen, and set out to tidy up His mangled Body, and wrap it decently, and put sweet-smelling things with it. If they can only get at it, which does not seem very likely. We know what utter astonishment awaited them.

Belief in the Resurrection is absolutely crucial for our faith; yet of all the articles of our belief, this is surely the hardest to accept in our time. But no Resurrection, no Christianity. As St Paul said, if we can't believe in that, in Christ's Resurrection and our own, the whole thing is useless. (Except as a system of ethics, he might have added.) Many of us find no difficulty in just taking God's word for it, and trusting to Him for the means.

What a splendid picture, the old idea of resurrection!

People emerging from their graves on the Last Day. I think at once of Stanley Spencer's great painting in the Tate Gallery; the lovely fresh brilliant morning in late April or early May; an ancient churchyard full of daffodils and hyacinths, and the dead pushing up their lids or bursting through the bright green turf – all in their best and smartest summer clothes. In all honesty, the kind of honesty we have now, we must leave that in the picture-books, and, if you must have some kind of image how it could possibly be true, we could turn to a very modern idea indeed – one that I heard in a recent broadcast. A star becomes unstable. It begins to collapse inwards under its own gravity. You might say it is crushing itself to death with its own weight. It goes on collapsing and shrinking until it is no size at all, while its gravity can only be put at infinity. This is an impossible state in the physical universe we know. So what happens next? They say it might disappear, that it might slip through this universe and into another. So there could be another universe to slip through into. Perhaps a great many other universes; I don't mean just other galaxies, but other whole creations. The theory may change. No doubt it will, but you see the idea; faith can always find a way onward. New concepts are always being presented which can be so used.

I'd like to end with a poetical image; an image no one could have had clearly in mind until man got off the earth, and stood out in space, and actually saw our planet as a globe; a revolving globe, with day on one side and night on the other. So beautiful; those tough men felt it to be the most moving sight.

There she goes on her ancient dance round the Sun, turning on herself, not monotonously, but swaying towards him and then away again, so that all the life on her gets a varying share of light and heat. The land-masses might be golden flesh, the oceans that cover most of her body a blue robe, the clouds that eddy continually about her seem like her white fleecy mantle. So far as we know, there is nothing like her; no other planet has her riches, her variety, her atmosphere. No other has that empty tomb.

Deepening Pleasures

1. Endeavour

G. O. NICKALLS

I'm often asked, 'Why on earth did you take up rowing?' 'Of all the . . .' and then my questioner breaks off. He simply hasn't the heart to thrust his cynical sword any further. My reasons are simple. Whether my activities have been concerned with rowing or painting, whether they have been crowned with success or failure, I have always derived the most intense pleasure from endeavour. At the age of six I was taken to see my father row at Henley. He was himself the outstandingly successful oarsman of his own and many other generations.

A few years ago, I wrote some lines in blank verse recalling my first day at Henley. I described it as

'A cornucopia of sights and sounds
A visual feast of quivering impressions!
Edwardian heyday, blue skies, pink champagne,
The razzle-dazzle of the parasol.'

Little did I know then the endeavour that would be required if I wanted to excel. And I did want to excel. Like hell I did.

Did I realise the months of hard training it involved? The forgoing of so many eating and drinking pleasures? The months of hard slogging, the improving of one's technique, the attainment of perfect synchronisation? All part of a dedicated endeavour.

If you happen to be captain, there are further responsibilities. With men training together day after day there is sure to be one member, perhaps two, who become the butt or butts of the rest of the crew. Now it is very important for a crew to live in harmony out of the boat. If they do not hit it off out of the boat, they are hardly likely to pull together in it. It is here that any captain worth his salt should make it his job to seek out the butt of the crew. Make a special friend of him and by the weight of his own personality draw him into the daily life of the crew so that he becomes something a good deal more than acceptable to the rest. This particular form of endeavour calls for a certain subtlety and sometimes a great deal of patience.

And then the race itself – joyous, determined and often very exhausting. Of course much more fun to win but even to lose has compensations if you know you have given of your best. But the sweet smell of victory, the knowledge that even though you may be behind at the time, you are going to win – sheer ecstasy – 'delighting as a giant to row your course' – the glorious, heady sensations of being, as Kipling wrote (in quite a different context I may say), 'drunk with sight of power'.

I mentioned painting just now. So far as I am concerned the delights of endeavour apply there, though in rather a different way. The determination of getting a picture to look as you want it to look; the struggles, the set-backs, the utter failures only too common so far as I am concerned. And then those rare and wonderful occasions when you attack the canvas in a fury of creation and it comes out just as you intended. Sheer bliss! Winston Churchill knew the feeling so well. In his book on painting he looked forward to an artist's life in the hereafter and imagined himself in a land of pure delight with all sorts of new and delicious colours to play around with. Nor was he alone in relishing the delights of endeavour. You may remember those lines on painting in another life:

'And they that were good shall be happy
They shall sit in a golden chair
And splash at a ten league canvas
With brushes of comets hair'   (Kipling)

Absolutely wonderful!

But to return to my first love – Henley Regatta. An old friend of mine, Woodgate, who was always known as 'Guts', died just over fifty years ago. He invented four-oared rowing without a cox, by the simple expedient of getting his cox to jump overboard on the word 'Go'. He was a winner of the Diamond Sculls and rowed eight races in one day over the Henley course – a fine example of endeavour. I attended his funeral with a concourse of old rowing men. Afterwards one Old Blue on returning home was greeted by his wife, 'Well,' she inquired, 'I suppose it was all very sad?' 'Sad?' he replied. 'Not a bit of it. We haven't had a better get-together since Henley Regatta.' And I think that's just how 'Guts' would have liked it.

2. The Wind's Eye
RICHARD MULKERN

It is an extraordinary thing for anybody to do. Most of the time you are damp, very uncomfortable, and a bit on edge. And yet there is a magic about sailing, about just being on the water, which is hard to describe.

The thought of two weeks cruising along the East Coast kept me going all through last winter. As I trudged through the slush and turned my collar up against the biting wind I dreamt of days to come with the wind running free and the sunlight dancing on the water. I dreamt of putting our noses out to sea, and reaching in again to spend nights ashore in the friendly pubs of small fishing villages. The months passed, the last few days of hectic activity, and we were away. Two men in a boat, leaving behind a sweltering countryside, a dock strike, and all the other unpleasant, irritating things of the land.

The wind stretched the sails into mathematically perfect arcs and the spray flew from the bows. We made the passage from the Crouch River to Harwich in record time. Six thirty in the morning and time to be away again to use the early tide. I poked my head out of the cabin. It was raining hard and there was the promise of more to come. Five days later we limped back into the Crouch; bedding soaked, tempers frayed, and no alternative but to cut short the cruise and slink home.

The difference between the dream and the reality. 'When I go on holiday . . .' Rivers, the seaside, power-boats, yachts. Getting your shoes off and feeling the sand trickling between your toes, feeling the wind in your hair, tasting the salt on your lips. The dream lingers on, and for me a part of the dream is sailing. Wind and water; the mixture is irresistible. I suppose you derive the same sort of satisfaction from climbing mountains, or just pottering about in the countryside when there's nobody about.

There *are* magic days. It is not always bad weather. It doesn't always rain – even in England. I've spent days on the water when I've thought, 'This is it. I'm there. There is a sense and a purpose, and I am part of it.'

Exhilarating moments when the rudder bites deep into the water and you are thrashing to windward in a Force five blow with all sails set and the water coming in green over the lee deck. Moments of tranquillity when, after a hard day's sailing, you anchor in some lovely inlet and go below to a snug cabin and hot food. Moments of peace.

Time spent on deck, drinking coffee and listening to the soft slap of the waves on the hull in the velvet darkness: gradually becoming aware of the world around. That's what it is all about really. Being aware. I often stay out on deck watching the stars, growing into the timeless universe, feeling a small part of God as I sit on my little boat looking out at a sky throbbing with life, telling me things about myself that I am only dimly aware of. But these moments of stillness are rare. The mood of the sea can change swiftly.

It was two years ago that it happened and I can remember the day as though it were yesterday. We were caught in the worst possible circumstances. Off the Crouch in a south-westerly and on a falling tide. You have heard that expression 'in the wind's eye'. Well, we were having to sail into it – or as near as we could get. A south-westerly which was tearing dead centre down the Crouch and roaring out into the estuary. We had reefed the mainsail and the storm jib was threatening to break free at any minute.

The wind was literally howling round our ears and short steep seas were breaking over the bows and hurling solid sheets of water the length of the boat. Three hours later, trembling, soaked to the skin and thankful to be alive, we anchored under the lee of the mainland, in the comparative shelter of the river.

Thankful to be alive. It is so easy to forget how close we are to death. The flick of a wheel when driving along and it could all be over in a few seconds. Going to sea, living close to the elements, reminds me of the realities of life – and death.

We need to take time out occasionally to get our bearings. There is a timeless quality, a primitive reality about the sea which shakes me out of my complacency to look again, into the eye of the wind.

3. Enjoying Silence
SHEILA CHICHESTER

I was educated at St Mary's School, Wantage. On Good Friday we kept silence all day until tea-time, and I really think we enjoyed it and it did us good. The day was well planned for us and at four o'clock we broke our silence with hot cross buns and felt that we had achieved something by this discipline.

One of the most wonderful experiences in my life was when I crossed the Atlantic alone with my husband in our yacht, Gipsy Moth Three. We sailed from New York to Plymouth and on our way we stopped at the Azores. This part of the passage was in beautiful weather with very smooth water and never will I forget the brilliant colours, and the moonlit nights and the star-studded skies which I used to sit in the cockpit and watch. When we landed in the Azores, at the tiny port called Horta, I was so impressed by the contrast of the people I saw there who were gentle and did not seem greedy and were very courteous. The contrast was enormous, after being in New York where there is so much bustle and money-making.

After we left the Azores it was late autumn and we had very rough weather indeed. Some of the waves were as much as quarter of a mile long, so it was not a violent movement, sitting in the cockpit, sliding down the waves. Watching these great seas roll, I seemed to feel the rhythm of the world; that this incredible globe we live in was turning and these waters swirling backwards and forwards drawn by the moon. The sea passage clears your mind of trivialities and at the same time gives you a great capacity for pleasure over small events, dolphins playing in the bow-wave or turtles swimming past. Away from the stress of modern life it is much easier to feel tranquil and happy and make good resolutions. But when you get back into the thick of it, keeping these things up and keeping calm, in touch with spiritual and non-material things, is very diffi-cult. I would suggest that fasting is a very good way to bring peace of mind. I am sure that businessmen, on whom we rely so much for the economy of this country and to get employment for many people, should take a day off, save expenses, and just fast and calm themselves down. In fact, I know of no better cure for restlessness than to have a fast – you get this wonderful peace of mind of renewed health and vitality. The trouble today is that most of us have got too far from the natural life.

When one returns from a long sea voyage, one is in a very natural state and is as one was meant to be, I think. You're enthusiastic, trusting and happy. In other words, after the calm and peace, your battery has been very much charged up, breathing the pure air, and so you are ready to give out to other people.

One of the things which I find gives me great peace of mind is listening to natural sounds as opposed to silence – such as sea sounds; particularly if you stay on an estuary and you hear the tide as it sucks its way out and then comes steadily in. I can remember when I was young and feeling very depressed, I used to stand on the seashore and when I saw this eternal rhythm of the sea coming in and sucking back, I felt that there was hope in life. Some of the ancient prayers thought out in stillness and solitude seem exactly right for today. One of my favourite prayers is St Augustine's, 'Thou hast made us for thyself, and our hearts are restless until they find rest in thee.'

4. Red Warning

TOM CROWE

We live in a Kentish farmhouse 400 years old. We are isolated. Our neighbours are the woods and fields. There is nearly always plenty to do, but one day when there wasn't, I and my son William, aged four, decided to try some magic. There was a clear blue sky except for one small black cloud across the sun. I told William that this was the right kind of day for magic. If we could find the spot that was the absolute dead centre of the wood, and stood there very still and gathered all our strength together, we could make anything happen. We would have magic in us.

So we set out. We crossed a big field and entered the wood. We said no word but walked slowly in, and soon we could no longer see the edge of the trees. 'How will we know when we find the magic place?' William asked.

'You'll feel a sudden stillness,' I said, 'and you'll be able to think the thought at the back of your mind that you could never quite think before. You'll feel the magic inside you.'

William put his hand in mine and we walked on, a little more slowly, further into the wood. Then we saw a small, mossy patch, quite smooth. We stood there. 'Here it is,' I said, 'this is the magic place. Stand still. Do you feel the magic?'

'Yes,' said William, 'I think I do.'

'Right. Now you have power over all the world, from the sky to the bottom of the sea. You can become whatever you like.'

'I'd like to be a tiger,' he said, 'but will I be able to get back to being myself again?'

'Yes, if you're careful.'

'Promise I'll be able to get back to myself. I want to go on being myself always.'

'Don't worry,' I said, 'so long as I'm with you you can always get back to yourself. Unless, of course, I turn into a tiger too by mistake – that would be a different matter. There might be nothing we could do about that.'

It's an old wood, this. The trees are tall. In summer it is dark. It was silent. So far as I was concerned, we were just filling in an afternoon, but to a small boy of four it was different. I suddenly realised that he was afraid. He flung his arms around my legs, buried his face in my knees, and said, 'Daddy, it *is* only a joke, isn't it?'

I had pushed things a little too far. What that little boy was afraid of losing was not his life, but something far more important and mysterious: he was afraid of losing *himself*.

Why is selfhood so critically important? If you think about it carefully it really is more important than mere life. I don't mean the Self that screams and snarls and bites when its vanity is wounded, I mean the one we meet less often – the Self that is stripped of all social, moral and intellectual pretensions. It confronts one at odd moments – perhaps when one's self-esteem has suffered; when one has let oneself down in some way, or let someone else down, which is the same thing. It's a rock-bottom place, firm ground at last, the only thing that makes each one of us unique in the Universe. I think it may have something to do with what the Irish poet Yeats refers to as 'radical innocence'. Those who have it make us feel good, however we may sneer or snigger when they have left our company. If we say something mean-spirited in their presence, we feel ourselves shrinking.

It's odd that something so valuable should be so little respected, in ourselves or in others. One is always hearing about the permissive society, but what worries me much more is its *dis*missiveness. We tend to dismiss every mystery, everything we don't quite understand, as unimportant, and forget about it. It's more comfortable that way. We are, to use Brendan Behan's phrase, 'daylight atheists' – until the plane is coming in to land in bumpy weather.

I grew up in the west of Ireland – a place where strangers still greet each other on the roads. Working as I now do in a big city, I am astonished at the way people who know each other don't even *see* each other as they pass in streets or corridors. I am a last-ditch individualist, a believer in the irreplaceable value of personality, and I feel that we're doing violence to this value in a frightening way.

There's an early warning system against nuclear attack. There are various alerts: 'Red Warnings', 'Grey Warnings', and so forth. But there are dangers other than those of nuclear weapons, and here is a Red Warning: I really believe that unless we recover some of our 'radical innocence', and the natural politeness and gaiety that stem from it, we may lose our capacity for happiness – long-term.

5. Darkness and Light

JASMINE ROSE-INNES

'Will it be winter soon?' my small daughter said to me this morning as she pulled on her thick tights by the heater in my bedroom. 'Oh, I hope not yet,' I said, a little shocked, I suppose, to realise how quickly the days are now drawing in. 'But I want it to be winter. I hope it will hurry up now. I can't wait for those long cosy evenings when we *do* things, and it's so smashing when it snows!' she said.

Now snow falls so seldom in London, and usually on weekdays, so that it's gone by the time the children are free to sledge and play in it – yet she loves winter! After she had dashed out to school I sat thinking about it as I drank my cup of tea. Why do we all have this instant negative reaction to the thought of winter, which makes us think in some regular cliché like, 'oh wretched winter, why can't it stay summer forever', because when I think about it I realise that I, like Joanna, am really looking forward to it. How tedious it would be if it were always summer. I'm sick of summer, and now can't wait for the flowers to die down beyond reprieve so that I can get on with the digging and clearing, to prepare for next spring. I look forward to seeing the different colours, shapes and contours of the land and the hills as they lie, spare and bony, without the padding, the monotony of universal green. I love the basic integrity of winter.

In West Africa where I have lived for many years, there were many times when I felt myself being continually worn away, depleted, by the sameness of so many equal days. Life was flowing out too fast without my being able to turn inward and regrow an inner stability. I had to come back to England to do that.

In winter we are, I think, more able to withdraw into a subconscious quietude wherein we can renew ourselves: think more slowly and clearly without the recurring pressures that summer puts upon us to be out and doing. Summer is a time for sun and sea and holidays and happy jaunts. But once again comes the time when the spiral of oneself needs to be secretly replenished – as in sleep.

Extroversion and introversion, summer and winter, darkness and light, how we need these contrasts and how fundamental they are to our balance and well-being.

Light and darkness; everywhere life is patterned with it. There are the smaller patterns of the day when things go fast or slow, and then the weeks can be swift flowing with pleasure or depressingly monotonous. Whole periods of life seem to go into tunnels of darkness when all seems negative and sad and no good and then suddenly patterns change and everything, that seemed difficult before, goes right.

Darkness and light, it is by these two opposites that everything is defined and has meaning. I am a photographer, among other things, and I also teach art, so I suppose I have become conditioned to a special awareness of everything around me. The full sunlight on a great chestnut tree can only show the massive spherical volume of its growth because it is cupped in deepest shadow, and bark – what incredible patterns of dark and light the sun chisels out of bark. So these patterns of darkness and light interweave in every direction. I think it was the psychologist Jung who interpreted the discrepancies in human behaviour by showing how the best and most high-minded of us has, deep within the subconscious mind, the darker shadow of a baser self. The brighter the light the darker the shadow, he contended. It is as though, having our roots in darkness, we are more able to reach the light.

When I really let myself think about it and begin to comprehend, I become almost dizzy with the beginnings of an understanding about how we are all held together by the rhythms and tensions of the opposites that control our spiralling universe. Introversion, extroversion, concave and convex, giving and receiving, sleeping and waking, darkness and light – I suppose this is why, in the dismay of these changing days, I am able to remain an optimist.

6. Light in Blindness
DAVID SCOTT BLACKHALL

All my light is remembered from the first forty-five years of my life. I have crammed the warehouse of my mind with visual memories and they are such good things to have, that there is no hint of wistfulness when I do some haphazard stocktaking. The light I remember most vividly is the first light of day in the shadow of the Snowdon Horseshoe. Most of the light we know is reflected light; we have to intercept it to be aware of it. We have to find a place for the light to fall on, and the first light of Snowdonia, new every morning and as old as the hills, has fallen on my memory and it keeps bouncing back. Some kind of mechanism in me, working under its own steam, has snatched at a minute fragment of time and made it immortal. At odd times I've looked at blue skies, flecked with a few casual puffs of cloud, and the vault of Heaven is now stuck like that forever. No summer has ever produced a sky so blue; never have wisps of cloud been so delicate as the ones my memory enhances. The light of the sky takes the giant's share of the light I remember but there is also the light I dream about.

Even when I am asleep, I am aware of the fact that I am blind – but I've had so long an acquaintance with seeing, that whatever I dream about is presented to me in visual terms. In my dreams I can see people, the streets, the meadows and the sky. I try to rationalise it and I tell myself in my dream that I can't really see it's some kind of trick, it's magic. It would be stupid for me to pretend that blindness is better than being able to see, and yet I know that in some ways I can see more clearly simply because I'm not distracted by those tricks which the light can play. All my life I have believed; it's stronger than belief – I know with dazzling certainty – that there is another kind of light which plays no tricks and which shines in the Sabbath of the heart. And the heart is a landscape which is also subject to darkness and light. But something tells me that this light will always be there when I want it, in a manner of speaking it is mine for the asking. And the crux of the matter is this – that we have to keep a place for the light to fall on; like the turning world itself, we make our own darkness by turning away from the source of everlasting light.

We need to remind ourselves that the landscape is always there. It was there before the daybreak discovered it; in the total darkness the landscape is there, the mountains and the sky are there. So many things have been there all the time and everyone has a special secret place in himself where the light can fall. I have no difficulty in believing that the sky is still there even though I can't see it. In some fields of human experience we have to begin by believing. This is the holy mountain where nothing can hurt or destroy. This is the light which can never be put out. The Psalmists had something to say on this subject and I feel that I have a special affinity with my illustrious namesake in the light of these words of 3000 years ago:

    'If I take the wings of the morning
    And dwell in the uttermost parts of the sea
    Even there shall Thy hand lead me and Thy right hand
       shall hold me
    If I say surely the darkness shall cover me
    Even the night shall be light about me
    Yea, the darkness hideth not from Thee
    But the night shineth as the day
    The darkness and the light are both alike to Thee.'